# EX LIBRIS

*My books are friends that never fail me*
THOMAS CARLYLE

# NATIONAL LIBRARY OF SCOTLAND
## Treasures Perpetual Diary

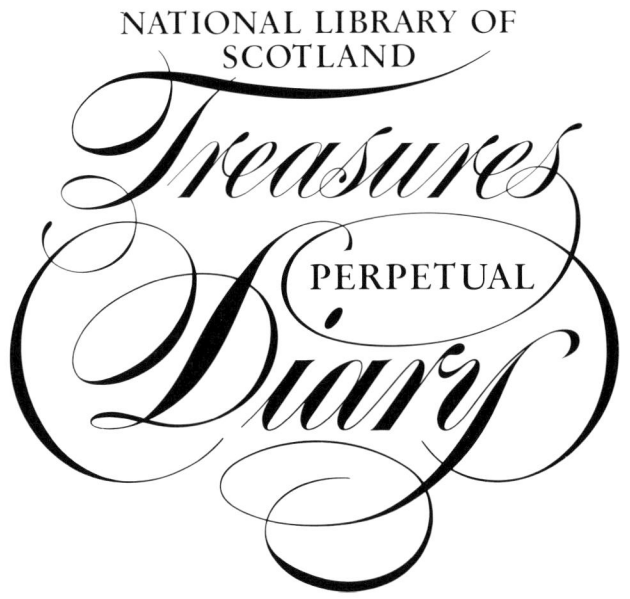

EDINBURGH: HMSO

*Cover illustration*
Roses, from Robert Thornton's superbly illustrated botanical work of the early 19th century.

*Frontispiece*
The royal arms of Scotland from the Lindsay Armorial, 1542.

Illustrations selected by Espeth Yeo National Library of Scotland.
Photography by Steve McAvoy National Library of Scotland.

© Crown copyright 1993
First published 1993
Application for reproduction should be made to HMSO
Designed by Graham Galloway
HMSO Graphic Design Edinburgh
ISBN 0 11 494236 6

HMSO publications are available from:

**HMSO Bookshops**
71 Lothian Road, Edinburgh, EH3 9AZ
031-228 4181 Fax 031-229 2734
49 High Holborn, London, WC1V 6HB
071-873 0011 Fax 071-873 8200 (counter service only)
258 Broad Street, Birmingham, B1 2HE
021-643 3740 Fax 021-643 6510
33 Wine Street, Bristol, BS1 2BQ
0272 264306 Fax 0272 294515
9-21 Princess Street, Manchester, M60 8AS
061-834 7201 Fax 061-833 0634
16 Arthur Street, Belfast, BT1 4GD
0232 238451 Fax 0232 235401

**HMSO Publications Centre**
(Mail, fax and telephone orders only)
PO Box 276, London, SW8 5DT
Telephone orders 071-873 9090
General enquiries 071-873 0011
(queuing system in operation for both numbers)
Fax orders 071-873 8200

**HMSO's Accredited Agents**
(see Yellow Pages)

*and through good booksellers*

# The National Library of Scotland
## Three Centuries of History

The National Library of Scotland was founded over 300 years ago as the Library of the Faculty of Advocates (the Scottish Bar). The Faculty has included Sir George Mackenzie of Rosehaugh, who was responsible for bringing the Library into being, James Boswell, Sir Walter Scott, Robert Louis Stevenson and other eminent Scots, and among the Keepers of its Library were Thomas Ruddiman and David Hume.

In 1710 the Copyright Act of Queen Anne entitled the Library to obtain a copy of every book published in Great Britain, a privilege that has been continued by later legislation. As the Library grew and became more famous it became the recognised repository of Scottish literary and historical manuscripts and of rare Scottish books, starting with the work of the first Scottish printers at the beginning of the 16th century. From its early days the Library also collected books in the main West European languages in the fields of history, literature, philosophy and related subjects.

Over the centuries the Advocates' Library developed into a national library in all but name, and eventually the upkeep of such a major collection proved too great a burden for a private body. In 1925, following the provision of an endowment by Sir Alexander Grant of Forres, the Government accepted the Faculty's offer to present its Library (with the exception of its legal books and manuscripts) to the nation. The National Library of Scotland was formally constituted by Act of Parliament in that year.

Part of the 'Magnum Opus', the interleaved set of the Waverley Novels made specially for Sir Walter Scott, which he used to correct and revise his work for the Magnum Edition of 1829–33.

# The National Library of Scotland Today

The National Library of Scotland is the largest library in Scotland and is among the six largest libraries in the British Isles. It houses over 6,000,000 printed items, as well as about 100,000 volumes of manuscripts and over 1,500,000 sheet maps. It takes some 20,000 current periodicals and newspaper titles, and each week around 6,500 printed items alone are added to stock.

Not surprisingly, the Library holds the most important collection of books and manuscripts relating to Scotland and the Scots, and attracts scholars and researchers from all over the world. It is also a major library for general research in all disciplines.

The Library's collections are as varied as they are large. Treasures include the last letter of Mary Queen of Scots, a Gutenberg Bible, and the most significant collection of Walter Scott material in the world. There is no shortage of serious works on everything from art to science, but there is also everyday material, from car manuals to theatre posters, children's comics and popular magazines. The manuscript collections include literary texts, correspondence, accounts of exploration and other journals and memoirs, political archives, and business papers, including estate records.

Services to readers are provided in all branches of the humanities and sciences, including business information, and in the specialist fields of music, maps, rare books and manuscripts. In this way, the Library provides for the needs of research, industry and commerce, and, by accumulating information about how we live now, safeguards the evidence of the present for future generations to study.

Only a small sample from the collections can be illustrated in this diary. Some of the items shown here are of international importance; some appear to be slight by comparison; but all are a part of Scotland's heritage which the Library is proud to preserve.

The devices of Walter Chepman and Andrew Myllar, who produced the earliest known Scottish books in 1508.

## 1993

**January**
S M T W T F S
               1 2
3 4 5 6 7 8 9
10 11 12 13 14 15 16
17 18 19 20 21 22 23
24 25 26 27 28 29 30
31

**February**
S M T W T F S
 1 2 3 4 5 6
7 8 9 10 11 12 13
14 15 16 17 18 19 20
21 22 23 24 25 26 27
28

**March**
S M T W T F S
 1 2 3 4 5 6
7 8 9 10 11 12 13
14 15 16 17 18 19 20
21 22 23 24 25 26 27
28 29 30 31

**April**
S M T W T F S
            1 2 3
4 5 6 7 8 9 10
11 12 13 14 15 16 17
18 19 20 21 22 23 24
25 26 27 28 29 30

**May**
S M T W T F S
                1
2 3 4 5 6 7 8
9 10 11 12 13 14 15
16 17 18 19 20 21 22
23 24 25 26 27 28 29
30 31

**June**
S M T W T F S
    1 2 3 4 5
6 7 8 9 10 11 12
13 14 15 16 17 18 19
20 21 22 23 24 25 26
27 28 29 30

**July**
S M T W T F S
         1 2 3
4 5 6 7 8 9 10
11 12 13 14 15 16 17
18 19 20 21 22 23 24
25 26 27 28 29 30 31

**August**
S M T W T F S
1 2 3 4 5 6 7
8 9 10 11 12 13 14
15 16 17 18 19 20 21
22 23 24 25 26 27 28
29 30 31

**September**
S M T W T F S
      1 2 3 4
5 6 7 8 9 10 11
12 13 14 15 16 17 18
19 20 21 22 23 24 25
26 27 28 29 30

**October**
S M T W T F S
             1 2
3 4 5 6 7 8 9
10 11 12 13 14 15 16
17 18 19 20 21 22 23
24 25 26 27 28 29 30
31

**November**
S M T W T F S
        1 2 3 4 5 6
7 8 9 10 11 12 13
14 15 16 17 18 19 20
21 22 23 24 25 26 27
28 29 30

**December**
S M T W T F S
       1 2 3 4
5 6 7 8 9 10 11
12 13 14 15 16 17 18
19 20 21 22 23 24 25
26 27 28 29 30 31

## 1994

**January**
S M T W T F S
                1
2 3 4 5 6 7 8
9 10 11 12 13 14 15
16 17 18 19 20 21 22
23 24 25 26 27 28 29
30 31

**February**
S M T W T F S
    1 2 3 4 5
6 7 8 9 10 11 12
13 14 15 16 17 18 19
20 21 22 23 24 25 26
27 28

**March**
S M T W T F S
    1 2 3 4 5
6 7 8 9 10 11 12
13 14 15 16 17 18 19
20 21 22 23 24 25 26
27 28 29 30 31

**April**
S M T W T F S
              1 2
3 4 5 6 7 8 9
10 11 12 13 14 15 16
17 18 19 20 21 22 23
24 25 26 27 28 29 30

**May**
S M T W T F S
1 2 3 4 5 6 7
8 9 10 11 12 13 14
15 16 17 18 19 20 21
22 23 24 25 26 27 28
29 30 31

**June**
S M T W T F S
        1 2 3 4
5 6 7 8 9 10 11
12 13 14 15 16 17 18
19 20 21 22 23 24 25
26 27 28 29 30

**July**
S M T W T F S
             1 2
3 4 5 6 7 8 9
10 11 12 13 14 15 16
17 18 19 20 21 22 23
24 25 26 27 28 29 30
31

**August**
S M T W T F S
 1 2 3 4 5 6
7 8 9 10 11 12 13
14 15 16 17 18 19 20
21 22 23 24 25 26 27
28 29 30 31

**September**
S M T W T F S
            1 2 3
4 5 6 7 8 9 10
11 12 13 14 15 16 17
18 19 20 21 22 23 24
25 26 27 28 29 30

**October**
S M T W T F S
                1
2 3 4 5 6 7 8
9 10 11 12 13 14 15
16 17 18 19 20 21 22
23 24 25 26 27 28 29
30 31

**November**
S M T W T F S
      1 2 3 4 5
6 7 8 9 10 11 12
13 14 15 16 17 18 19
20 21 22 23 24 25 26
27 28 29 30

**December**
S M T W T F S
            1 2 3
4 5 6 7 8 9 10
11 12 13 14 15 16 17
18 19 20 21 22 23 24
25 26 27 28 29 30 31

# 1995

### January
| S | M | T | W | T | F | S |
|---|---|---|---|---|---|---|
| 1 | 2 | 3 | 4 | 5 | 6 | 7 |
| 8 | 9 | 10 | 11 | 12 | 13 | 14 |
| 15 | 16 | 17 | 18 | 19 | 20 | 21 |
| 22 | 23 | 24 | 25 | 26 | 27 | 28 |
| 29 | 30 | 31 | | | | |

### February
| S | M | T | W | T | F | S |
|---|---|---|---|---|---|---|
| | | | 1 | 2 | 3 | 4 |
| 5 | 6 | 7 | 8 | 9 | 10 | 11 |
| 12 | 13 | 14 | 15 | 16 | 17 | 18 |
| 19 | 20 | 21 | 22 | 23 | 24 | 25 |
| 26 | 27 | 28 | | | | |

### March
| S | M | T | W | T | F | S |
|---|---|---|---|---|---|---|
| | | | 1 | 2 | 3 | 4 |
| 5 | 6 | 7 | 8 | 9 | 10 | 11 |
| 12 | 13 | 14 | 15 | 16 | 17 | 18 |
| 19 | 20 | 21 | 22 | 23 | 24 | 25 |
| 26 | 27 | 28 | 29 | 30 | 31 | |

### April
| S | M | T | W | T | F | S |
|---|---|---|---|---|---|---|
| | | | | | | 1 |
| 2 | 3 | 4 | 5 | 6 | 7 | 8 |
| 9 | 10 | 11 | 12 | 13 | 14 | 15 |
| 16 | 17 | 18 | 19 | 20 | 21 | 22 |
| 23 | 24 | 25 | 26 | 27 | 28 | 29 |
| 30 | | | | | | |

### May
| S | M | T | W | T | F | S |
|---|---|---|---|---|---|---|
| | 1 | 2 | 3 | 4 | 5 | 6 |
| 7 | 8 | 9 | 10 | 11 | 12 | 13 |
| 14 | 15 | 16 | 17 | 18 | 19 | 20 |
| 21 | 22 | 23 | 24 | 25 | 26 | 27 |
| 28 | 29 | 30 | 31 | | | |

### June
| S | M | T | W | T | F | S |
|---|---|---|---|---|---|---|
| | | | | 1 | 2 | 3 |
| 4 | 5 | 6 | 7 | 8 | 9 | 10 |
| 11 | 12 | 13 | 14 | 15 | 16 | 17 |
| 18 | 19 | 20 | 21 | 22 | 23 | 24 |
| 25 | 26 | 27 | 28 | 29 | 30 | |

### July
| S | M | T | W | T | F | S |
|---|---|---|---|---|---|---|
| | | | | | | 1 |
| 2 | 3 | 4 | 5 | 6 | 7 | 8 |
| 9 | 10 | 11 | 12 | 13 | 14 | 15 |
| 16 | 17 | 18 | 19 | 20 | 21 | 22 |
| 23 | 24 | 25 | 26 | 27 | 28 | 29 |
| 30 | 31 | | | | | |

### August
| S | M | T | W | T | F | S |
|---|---|---|---|---|---|---|
| | | 1 | 2 | 3 | 4 | 5 |
| 6 | 7 | 8 | 9 | 10 | 11 | 12 |
| 13 | 14 | 15 | 16 | 17 | 18 | 19 |
| 20 | 21 | 22 | 23 | 24 | 25 | 26 |
| 27 | 28 | 29 | 30 | 31 | | |

### September
| S | M | T | W | T | F | S |
|---|---|---|---|---|---|---|
| | | | | | 1 | 2 |
| 3 | 4 | 5 | 6 | 7 | 8 | 9 |
| 10 | 11 | 12 | 13 | 14 | 15 | 16 |
| 17 | 18 | 19 | 20 | 21 | 22 | 23 |
| 24 | 25 | 26 | 27 | 28 | 29 | 30 |

### October
| S | M | T | W | T | F | S |
|---|---|---|---|---|---|---|
| 1 | 2 | 3 | 4 | 5 | 6 | 7 |
| 8 | 9 | 10 | 11 | 12 | 13 | 14 |
| 15 | 16 | 17 | 18 | 19 | 20 | 21 |
| 22 | 23 | 24 | 25 | 26 | 27 | 28 |
| 29 | 30 | 31 | | | | |

### November
| S | M | T | W | T | F | S |
|---|---|---|---|---|---|---|
| | | | 1 | 2 | 3 | 4 |
| 5 | 6 | 7 | 8 | 9 | 10 | 11 |
| 12 | 13 | 14 | 15 | 16 | 17 | 18 |
| 19 | 20 | 21 | 22 | 23 | 24 | 25 |
| 26 | 27 | 28 | 29 | 30 | | |

### December
| S | M | T | W | T | F | S |
|---|---|---|---|---|---|---|
| | | | | | 1 | 2 |
| 3 | 4 | 5 | 6 | 7 | 8 | 9 |
| 10 | 11 | 12 | 13 | 14 | 15 | 16 |
| 17 | 18 | 19 | 20 | 21 | 22 | 23 |
| 24 | 25 | 26 | 27 | 28 | 29 | 30 |
| 31 | | | | | | |

# 1996 leap year

### January
| S | M | T | W | T | F | S |
|---|---|---|---|---|---|---|
| | 1 | 2 | 3 | 4 | 5 | 6 |
| 7 | 8 | 9 | 10 | 11 | 12 | 13 |
| 14 | 15 | 16 | 17 | 18 | 19 | 20 |
| 21 | 22 | 23 | 24 | 25 | 26 | 27 |
| 28 | 29 | 30 | 31 | | | |

### February
| S | M | T | W | T | F | S |
|---|---|---|---|---|---|---|
| | | | | 1 | 2 | 3 |
| 4 | 5 | 6 | 7 | 8 | 9 | 10 |
| 11 | 12 | 13 | 14 | 15 | 16 | 17 |
| 18 | 19 | 20 | 21 | 22 | 23 | 24 |
| 25 | 26 | 27 | 28 | 29 | | |

### March
| S | M | T | W | T | F | S |
|---|---|---|---|---|---|---|
| | | | | | 1 | 2 |
| 3 | 4 | 5 | 6 | 7 | 8 | 9 |
| 10 | 11 | 12 | 13 | 14 | 15 | 16 |
| 17 | 18 | 19 | 20 | 21 | 22 | 23 |
| 24 | 25 | 26 | 27 | 28 | 29 | 30 |
| 31 | | | | | | |

### April
| S | M | T | W | T | F | S |
|---|---|---|---|---|---|---|
| | 1 | 2 | 3 | 4 | 5 | 6 |
| 7 | 8 | 9 | 10 | 11 | 12 | 13 |
| 14 | 15 | 16 | 17 | 18 | 19 | 20 |
| 21 | 22 | 23 | 24 | 25 | 26 | 27 |
| 28 | 29 | 30 | | | | |

### May
| S | M | T | W | T | F | S |
|---|---|---|---|---|---|---|
| | | | 1 | 2 | 3 | 4 |
| 5 | 6 | 7 | 8 | 9 | 10 | 11 |
| 12 | 13 | 14 | 15 | 16 | 17 | 18 |
| 19 | 20 | 21 | 22 | 23 | 24 | 25 |
| 26 | 27 | 28 | 29 | 30 | 31 | |

### June
| S | M | T | W | T | F | S |
|---|---|---|---|---|---|---|
| | | | | | | 1 |
| 2 | 3 | 4 | 5 | 6 | 7 | 8 |
| 9 | 10 | 11 | 12 | 13 | 14 | 15 |
| 16 | 17 | 18 | 19 | 20 | 21 | 22 |
| 23 | 24 | 25 | 26 | 27 | 28 | 29 |
| 30 | | | | | | |

### July
| S | M | T | W | T | F | S |
|---|---|---|---|---|---|---|
| | 1 | 2 | 3 | 4 | 5 | 6 |
| 7 | 8 | 9 | 10 | 11 | 12 | 13 |
| 14 | 15 | 16 | 17 | 18 | 19 | 20 |
| 21 | 22 | 23 | 24 | 25 | 26 | 27 |
| 28 | 29 | 30 | 31 | | | |

### August
| S | M | T | W | T | F | S |
|---|---|---|---|---|---|---|
| | | | | 1 | 2 | 3 |
| 4 | 5 | 6 | 7 | 8 | 9 | 10 |
| 11 | 12 | 13 | 14 | 15 | 16 | 17 |
| 18 | 19 | 20 | 21 | 22 | 23 | 24 |
| 25 | 26 | 27 | 28 | 29 | 30 | 31 |

### September
| S | M | T | W | T | F | S |
|---|---|---|---|---|---|---|
| 1 | 2 | 3 | 4 | 5 | 6 | 7 |
| 8 | 9 | 10 | 11 | 12 | 13 | 14 |
| 15 | 16 | 17 | 18 | 19 | 20 | 21 |
| 22 | 23 | 24 | 25 | 26 | 27 | 28 |
| 29 | 30 | | | | | |

### October
| S | M | T | W | T | F | S |
|---|---|---|---|---|---|---|
| | | 1 | 2 | 3 | 4 | 5 |
| 6 | 7 | 8 | 9 | 10 | 11 | 12 |
| 13 | 14 | 15 | 16 | 17 | 18 | 19 |
| 20 | 21 | 22 | 23 | 24 | 25 | 26 |
| 27 | 28 | 29 | 30 | 31 | | |

### November
| S | M | T | W | T | F | S |
|---|---|---|---|---|---|---|
| | | | | | 1 | 2 |
| 3 | 4 | 5 | 6 | 7 | 8 | 9 |
| 10 | 11 | 12 | 13 | 14 | 15 | 16 |
| 17 | 18 | 19 | 20 | 21 | 22 | 23 |
| 24 | 25 | 26 | 27 | 28 | 29 | 30 |

### December
| S | M | T | W | T | F | S |
|---|---|---|---|---|---|---|
| 1 | 2 | 3 | 4 | 5 | 6 | 7 |
| 8 | 9 | 10 | 11 | 12 | 13 | 14 |
| 15 | 16 | 17 | 18 | 19 | 20 | 21 |
| 22 | 23 | 24 | 25 | 26 | 27 | 28 |
| 29 | 30 | 31 | | | | |

## 1997

| January | | | | | | | February | | | | | | | March | | | | | | | April | | | | | | |
|---|---|---|---|---|---|---|---|---|---|---|---|---|---|---|---|---|---|---|---|---|---|---|---|---|---|---|---|
| S | M | T | W | T | F | S | S | M | T | W | T | F | S | S | M | T | W | T | F | S | S | M | T | W | T | F | S |
|   |   |   | 1 | 2 | 3 | 4 |   |   |   |   |   |   | 1 |   |   |   |   |   |   | 1 |   |   | 1 | 2 | 3 | 4 | 5 |
| 5 | 6 | 7 | 8 | 9 | 10 | 11 | 2 | 3 | 4 | 5 | 6 | 7 | 8 | 2 | 3 | 4 | 5 | 6 | 7 | 8 | 6 | 7 | 8 | 9 | 10 | 11 | 12 |
| 12 | 13 | 14 | 15 | 16 | 17 | 18 | 9 | 10 | 11 | 12 | 13 | 14 | 15 | 9 | 10 | 11 | 12 | 13 | 14 | 15 | 13 | 14 | 15 | 16 | 17 | 18 | 19 |
| 19 | 20 | 21 | 22 | 23 | 24 | 25 | 16 | 17 | 18 | 19 | 20 | 21 | 22 | 16 | 17 | 18 | 19 | 20 | 21 | 22 | 20 | 21 | 22 | 23 | 24 | 25 | 26 |
| 26 | 27 | 28 | 29 | 30 | 31 |   | 23 | 24 | 25 | 26 | 27 | 28 |   | 23 | 24 | 25 | 26 | 27 | 28 | 29 | 27 | 28 | 29 | 30 |   |   |   |
|   |   |   |   |   |   |   |   |   |   |   |   |   |   | 30 | 31 |   |   |   |   |   |   |   |   |   |   |   |   |

| May | | | | | | | June | | | | | | | July | | | | | | | August | | | | | | |
|---|---|---|---|---|---|---|---|---|---|---|---|---|---|---|---|---|---|---|---|---|---|---|---|---|---|---|---|
| S | M | T | W | T | F | S | S | M | T | W | T | F | S | S | M | T | W | T | F | S | S | M | T | W | T | F | S |
|   |   |   |   | 1 | 2 | 3 | 1 | 2 | 3 | 4 | 5 | 6 | 7 |   |   | 1 | 2 | 3 | 4 | 5 |   |   |   |   |   | 1 | 2 |
| 4 | 5 | 6 | 7 | 8 | 9 | 10 | 8 | 9 | 10 | 11 | 12 | 13 | 14 | 6 | 7 | 8 | 9 | 10 | 11 | 12 | 3 | 4 | 5 | 6 | 7 | 8 | 9 |
| 11 | 12 | 13 | 14 | 15 | 16 | 17 | 15 | 16 | 17 | 18 | 19 | 20 | 21 | 13 | 14 | 15 | 16 | 17 | 18 | 19 | 10 | 11 | 12 | 13 | 14 | 15 | 16 |
| 18 | 19 | 20 | 21 | 22 | 23 | 24 | 22 | 23 | 24 | 25 | 26 | 27 | 28 | 20 | 21 | 22 | 23 | 24 | 25 | 26 | 17 | 18 | 19 | 20 | 21 | 22 | 23 |
| 25 | 26 | 27 | 28 | 29 | 30 | 31 | 29 | 30 |   |   |   |   |   | 27 | 28 | 29 | 30 | 31 |   |   | 24 | 25 | 26 | 27 | 28 | 29 | 30 |
|   |   |   |   |   |   |   |   |   |   |   |   |   |   |   |   |   |   |   |   |   | 31 |   |   |   |   |   |   |

| September | | | | | | | October | | | | | | | November | | | | | | | December | | | | | | |
|---|---|---|---|---|---|---|---|---|---|---|---|---|---|---|---|---|---|---|---|---|---|---|---|---|---|---|---|
| S | M | T | W | T | F | S | S | M | T | W | T | F | S | S | M | T | W | T | F | S | S | M | T | W | T | F | S |
|   | 1 | 2 | 3 | 4 | 5 | 6 |   |   |   | 1 | 2 | 3 | 4 |   |   |   |   |   |   | 1 |   | 1 | 2 | 3 | 4 | 5 | 6 |
| 7 | 8 | 9 | 10 | 11 | 12 | 13 | 5 | 6 | 7 | 8 | 9 | 10 | 11 | 2 | 3 | 4 | 5 | 6 | 7 | 8 | 7 | 8 | 9 | 10 | 11 | 12 | 13 |
| 14 | 15 | 16 | 17 | 18 | 19 | 20 | 12 | 13 | 14 | 15 | 16 | 17 | 18 | 9 | 10 | 11 | 12 | 13 | 14 | 15 | 14 | 15 | 16 | 17 | 18 | 19 | 20 |
| 21 | 22 | 23 | 24 | 25 | 26 | 27 | 19 | 20 | 21 | 22 | 23 | 24 | 25 | 16 | 17 | 18 | 19 | 20 | 21 | 22 | 21 | 22 | 23 | 24 | 25 | 26 | 27 |
| 28 | 29 | 30 |   |   |   |   | 26 | 27 | 28 | 29 | 30 | 31 |   | 23 | 24 | 25 | 26 | 27 | 28 | 29 | 28 | 29 | 30 | 31 |   |   |   |
|   |   |   |   |   |   |   |   |   |   |   |   |   |   | 30 |   |   |   |   |   |   |   |   |   |   |   |   |   |

## 1998

| January | | | | | | | February | | | | | | | March | | | | | | | April | | | | | | |
|---|---|---|---|---|---|---|---|---|---|---|---|---|---|---|---|---|---|---|---|---|---|---|---|---|---|---|---|
| S | M | T | W | T | F | S | S | M | T | W | T | F | S | S | M | T | W | T | F | S | S | M | T | W | T | F | S |
|   |   |   |   | 1 | 2 | 3 | 1 | 2 | 3 | 4 | 5 | 6 | 7 | 1 | 2 | 3 | 4 | 5 | 6 | 7 |   |   |   | 1 | 2 | 3 | 4 |
| 4 | 5 | 6 | 7 | 8 | 9 | 10 | 8 | 9 | 10 | 11 | 12 | 13 | 14 | 8 | 9 | 10 | 11 | 12 | 13 | 14 | 5 | 6 | 7 | 8 | 9 | 10 | 11 |
| 11 | 12 | 13 | 14 | 15 | 16 | 17 | 15 | 16 | 17 | 18 | 19 | 20 | 21 | 15 | 16 | 17 | 18 | 19 | 20 | 21 | 12 | 13 | 14 | 15 | 16 | 17 | 18 |
| 18 | 19 | 20 | 21 | 22 | 23 | 24 | 22 | 23 | 24 | 25 | 26 | 27 | 28 | 22 | 23 | 24 | 25 | 26 | 27 | 28 | 19 | 20 | 21 | 22 | 23 | 24 | 25 |
| 25 | 26 | 27 | 28 | 29 | 30 | 31 |   |   |   |   |   |   |   | 29 | 30 | 31 |   |   |   |   | 26 | 27 | 28 | 29 | 30 |   |   |

| May | | | | | | | June | | | | | | | July | | | | | | | August | | | | | | |
|---|---|---|---|---|---|---|---|---|---|---|---|---|---|---|---|---|---|---|---|---|---|---|---|---|---|---|---|
| S | M | T | W | T | F | S | S | M | T | W | T | F | S | S | M | T | W | T | F | S | S | M | T | W | T | F | S |
|   |   |   |   |   | 1 | 2 |   | 1 | 2 | 3 | 4 | 5 | 6 |   |   |   | 1 | 2 | 3 | 4 |   |   |   |   |   |   | 1 |
| 3 | 4 | 5 | 6 | 7 | 8 | 9 | 7 | 8 | 9 | 10 | 11 | 12 | 13 | 5 | 6 | 7 | 8 | 9 | 10 | 11 | 2 | 3 | 4 | 5 | 6 | 7 | 8 |
| 10 | 11 | 12 | 13 | 14 | 15 | 16 | 14 | 15 | 16 | 17 | 18 | 19 | 20 | 12 | 13 | 14 | 15 | 16 | 17 | 18 | 9 | 10 | 11 | 12 | 13 | 14 | 15 |
| 17 | 18 | 19 | 20 | 21 | 22 | 23 | 21 | 22 | 23 | 24 | 25 | 26 | 27 | 19 | 20 | 21 | 22 | 23 | 24 | 25 | 16 | 17 | 18 | 19 | 20 | 21 | 22 |
| 24 | 25 | 26 | 27 | 28 | 29 | 30 | 28 | 29 | 30 |   |   |   |   | 26 | 27 | 28 | 29 | 30 | 31 |   | 23 | 24 | 25 | 26 | 27 | 28 | 29 |
| 31 |   |   |   |   |   |   |   |   |   |   |   |   |   |   |   |   |   |   |   |   | 30 | 31 |   |   |   |   |   |

| September | | | | | | | October | | | | | | | November | | | | | | | December | | | | | | |
|---|---|---|---|---|---|---|---|---|---|---|---|---|---|---|---|---|---|---|---|---|---|---|---|---|---|---|---|
| S | M | T | W | T | F | S | S | M | T | W | T | F | S | S | M | T | W | T | F | S | S | M | T | W | T | F | S |
|   |   | 1 | 2 | 3 | 4 | 5 |   |   |   |   | 1 | 2 | 3 | 1 | 2 | 3 | 4 | 5 | 6 | 7 |   |   | 1 | 2 | 3 | 4 | 5 |
| 6 | 7 | 8 | 9 | 10 | 11 | 12 | 4 | 5 | 6 | 7 | 8 | 9 | 10 | 8 | 9 | 10 | 11 | 12 | 13 | 14 | 6 | 7 | 8 | 9 | 10 | 11 | 12 |
| 13 | 14 | 15 | 16 | 17 | 18 | 19 | 11 | 12 | 13 | 14 | 15 | 16 | 17 | 15 | 16 | 17 | 18 | 19 | 20 | 21 | 13 | 14 | 15 | 16 | 17 | 18 | 19 |
| 20 | 21 | 22 | 23 | 24 | 25 | 26 | 18 | 19 | 20 | 21 | 22 | 23 | 24 | 22 | 23 | 24 | 25 | 26 | 27 | 28 | 20 | 21 | 22 | 23 | 24 | 25 | 26 |
| 27 | 28 | 29 | 30 |   |   |   | 25 | 26 | 27 | 28 | 29 | 30 | 31 | 29 | 30 |   |   |   |   |   | 27 | 28 | 29 | 30 | 31 |   |   |

## 1999

### January
| S | M | T | W | T | F | S |
|---|---|---|---|---|---|---|
|   |   |   |   |   | 1 | 2 |
| 3 | 4 | 5 | 6 | 7 | 8 | 9 |
| 10 | 11 | 12 | 13 | 14 | 15 | 16 |
| 17 | 18 | 19 | 20 | 21 | 22 | 23 |
| 24 | 25 | 26 | 27 | 28 | 29 | 30 |
| 31 |   |   |   |   |   |   |

### February
| S | M | T | W | T | F | S |
|---|---|---|---|---|---|---|
|   | 1 | 2 | 3 | 4 | 5 | 6 |
| 7 | 8 | 9 | 10 | 11 | 12 | 13 |
| 14 | 15 | 16 | 17 | 18 | 19 | 20 |
| 21 | 22 | 23 | 24 | 25 | 26 | 27 |
| 28 |   |   |   |   |   |   |

### March
| S | M | T | W | T | F | S |
|---|---|---|---|---|---|---|
|   | 1 | 2 | 3 | 4 | 5 | 6 |
| 7 | 8 | 9 | 10 | 11 | 12 | 13 |
| 14 | 15 | 16 | 17 | 18 | 19 | 20 |
| 21 | 22 | 23 | 24 | 25 | 26 | 27 |
| 28 | 29 | 30 | 31 |   |   |   |

### April
| S | M | T | W | T | F | S |
|---|---|---|---|---|---|---|
|   |   |   |   | 1 | 2 | 3 |
| 4 | 5 | 6 | 7 | 8 | 9 | 10 |
| 11 | 12 | 13 | 14 | 15 | 16 | 17 |
| 18 | 19 | 20 | 21 | 22 | 23 | 24 |
| 25 | 26 | 27 | 28 | 29 | 30 |   |

### May
| S | M | T | W | T | F | S |
|---|---|---|---|---|---|---|
|   |   |   |   |   |   | 1 |
| 2 | 3 | 4 | 5 | 6 | 7 | 8 |
| 9 | 10 | 11 | 12 | 13 | 14 | 15 |
| 16 | 17 | 18 | 19 | 20 | 21 | 22 |
| 23 | 24 | 25 | 26 | 27 | 28 | 29 |
| 30 | 31 |   |   |   |   |   |

### June
| S | M | T | W | T | F | S |
|---|---|---|---|---|---|---|
|   |   | 1 | 2 | 3 | 4 | 5 |
| 6 | 7 | 8 | 9 | 10 | 11 | 12 |
| 13 | 14 | 15 | 16 | 17 | 18 | 19 |
| 20 | 21 | 22 | 23 | 24 | 25 | 26 |
| 27 | 28 | 29 | 30 |   |   |   |

### July
| S | M | T | W | T | F | S |
|---|---|---|---|---|---|---|
|   |   |   |   | 1 | 2 | 3 |
| 4 | 5 | 6 | 7 | 8 | 9 | 10 |
| 11 | 12 | 13 | 14 | 15 | 16 | 17 |
| 18 | 19 | 20 | 21 | 22 | 23 | 24 |
| 25 | 26 | 27 | 28 | 29 | 30 | 31 |

### August
| S | M | T | W | T | F | S |
|---|---|---|---|---|---|---|
| 1 | 2 | 3 | 4 | 5 | 6 | 7 |
| 8 | 9 | 10 | 11 | 12 | 13 | 14 |
| 15 | 16 | 17 | 18 | 19 | 20 | 21 |
| 22 | 23 | 24 | 25 | 26 | 27 | 28 |
| 29 | 30 | 31 |   |   |   |   |

### September
| S | M | T | W | T | F | S |
|---|---|---|---|---|---|---|
|   |   |   | 1 | 2 | 3 | 4 |
| 5 | 6 | 7 | 8 | 9 | 10 | 11 |
| 12 | 13 | 14 | 15 | 16 | 17 | 18 |
| 19 | 20 | 21 | 22 | 23 | 24 | 25 |
| 26 | 27 | 28 | 29 | 30 |   |   |

### October
| S | M | T | W | T | F | S |
|---|---|---|---|---|---|---|
|   |   |   |   |   | 1 | 2 |
| 3 | 4 | 5 | 6 | 7 | 8 | 9 |
| 10 | 11 | 12 | 13 | 14 | 15 | 16 |
| 17 | 18 | 19 | 20 | 21 | 22 | 23 |
| 24 | 25 | 26 | 27 | 28 | 29 | 30 |
| 31 |   |   |   |   |   |   |

### November
| S | M | T | W | T | F | S |
|---|---|---|---|---|---|---|
|   | 1 | 2 | 3 | 4 | 5 | 6 |
| 7 | 8 | 9 | 10 | 11 | 12 | 13 |
| 14 | 15 | 16 | 17 | 18 | 19 | 20 |
| 21 | 22 | 23 | 24 | 25 | 26 | 27 |
| 28 | 29 | 30 |   |   |   |   |

### December
| S | M | T | W | T | F | S |
|---|---|---|---|---|---|---|
|   |   |   | 1 | 2 | 3 | 4 |
| 5 | 6 | 7 | 8 | 9 | 10 | 11 |
| 12 | 13 | 14 | 15 | 16 | 17 | 18 |
| 19 | 20 | 21 | 22 | 23 | 24 | 25 |
| 26 | 27 | 28 | 29 | 30 | 31 |   |

## 2000 leap year

### January
| S | M | T | W | T | F | S |
|---|---|---|---|---|---|---|
|   |   |   |   |   |   | 1 |
| 2 | 3 | 4 | 5 | 6 | 7 | 8 |
| 9 | 10 | 11 | 12 | 13 | 14 | 15 |
| 16 | 17 | 18 | 19 | 20 | 21 | 22 |
| 23 | 24 | 25 | 26 | 27 | 28 | 29 |
| 30 | 31 |   |   |   |   |   |

### February
| S | M | T | W | T | F | S |
|---|---|---|---|---|---|---|
|   |   | 1 | 2 | 3 | 4 | 5 |
| 6 | 7 | 8 | 9 | 10 | 11 | 12 |
| 13 | 14 | 15 | 16 | 17 | 18 | 19 |
| 20 | 21 | 22 | 23 | 24 | 25 | 26 |
| 27 | 28 | 29 |   |   |   |   |

### March
| S | M | T | W | T | F | S |
|---|---|---|---|---|---|---|
|   |   |   | 1 | 2 | 3 | 4 |
| 5 | 6 | 7 | 8 | 9 | 10 | 11 |
| 12 | 13 | 14 | 15 | 16 | 17 | 18 |
| 19 | 20 | 21 | 22 | 23 | 24 | 25 |
| 26 | 27 | 28 | 29 | 30 | 31 |   |

### April
| S | M | T | W | T | F | S |
|---|---|---|---|---|---|---|
|   |   |   |   |   |   | 1 |
| 2 | 3 | 4 | 5 | 6 | 7 | 8 |
| 9 | 10 | 11 | 12 | 13 | 14 | 15 |
| 16 | 17 | 18 | 19 | 20 | 21 | 22 |
| 23 | 24 | 25 | 26 | 27 | 28 | 29 |
| 30 |   |   |   |   |   |   |

### May
| S | M | T | W | T | F | S |
|---|---|---|---|---|---|---|
|   | 1 | 2 | 3 | 4 | 5 | 6 |
| 7 | 8 | 9 | 10 | 11 | 12 | 13 |
| 14 | 15 | 16 | 17 | 18 | 19 | 20 |
| 21 | 22 | 23 | 24 | 25 | 26 | 27 |
| 28 | 29 | 30 | 31 |   |   |   |

### June
| S | M | T | W | T | F | S |
|---|---|---|---|---|---|---|
|   |   |   |   | 1 | 2 | 3 |
| 4 | 5 | 6 | 7 | 8 | 9 | 10 |
| 11 | 12 | 13 | 14 | 15 | 16 | 17 |
| 18 | 19 | 20 | 21 | 22 | 23 | 24 |
| 25 | 26 | 27 | 28 | 29 | 30 |   |

### July
| S | M | T | W | T | F | S |
|---|---|---|---|---|---|---|
|   |   |   |   |   |   | 1 |
| 2 | 3 | 4 | 5 | 6 | 7 | 8 |
| 9 | 10 | 11 | 12 | 13 | 14 | 15 |
| 16 | 17 | 18 | 19 | 20 | 21 | 22 |
| 23 | 24 | 25 | 26 | 27 | 28 | 29 |
| 30 | 31 |   |   |   |   |   |

### August
| S | M | T | W | T | F | S |
|---|---|---|---|---|---|---|
|   |   | 1 | 2 | 3 | 4 | 5 |
| 6 | 7 | 8 | 9 | 10 | 11 | 12 |
| 13 | 14 | 15 | 16 | 17 | 18 | 19 |
| 20 | 21 | 22 | 23 | 24 | 25 | 26 |
| 27 | 28 | 29 | 30 | 31 |   |   |

### September
| S | M | T | W | T | F | S |
|---|---|---|---|---|---|---|
|   |   |   |   |   | 1 | 2 |
| 3 | 4 | 5 | 6 | 7 | 8 | 9 |
| 10 | 11 | 12 | 13 | 14 | 15 | 16 |
| 17 | 18 | 19 | 20 | 21 | 22 | 23 |
| 24 | 25 | 26 | 27 | 28 | 29 | 30 |

### October
| S | M | T | W | T | F | S |
|---|---|---|---|---|---|---|
| 1 | 2 | 3 | 4 | 5 | 6 | 7 |
| 8 | 9 | 10 | 11 | 12 | 13 | 14 |
| 15 | 16 | 17 | 18 | 19 | 20 | 21 |
| 22 | 23 | 24 | 25 | 26 | 27 | 28 |
| 29 | 30 | 31 |   |   |   |   |

### November
| S | M | T | W | T | F | S |
|---|---|---|---|---|---|---|
|   |   |   | 1 | 2 | 3 | 4 |
| 5 | 6 | 7 | 8 | 9 | 10 | 11 |
| 12 | 13 | 14 | 15 | 16 | 17 | 18 |
| 19 | 20 | 21 | 22 | 23 | 24 | 25 |
| 26 | 27 | 28 | 29 | 30 |   |   |

### December
| S | M | T | W | T | F | S |
|---|---|---|---|---|---|---|
|   |   |   |   |   | 1 | 2 |
| 3 | 4 | 5 | 6 | 7 | 8 | 9 |
| 10 | 11 | 12 | 13 | 14 | 15 | 16 |
| 17 | 18 | 19 | 20 | 21 | 22 | 23 |
| 24 | 25 | 26 | 27 | 28 | 29 | 30 |
| 31 |   |   |   |   |   |   |

# Birthdays & Anniversaries

# Birthdays & Anniversaries

# January

1

2

3

4

5

6

7

A Victorian greetings card, c.1870.

*Previous page*. Detail from a portolan (a sea chart) of the Mediterranean by the Cretan chartmaker Georgio Calapoda, 1560.

# January

8

9

10

11

12

13

14

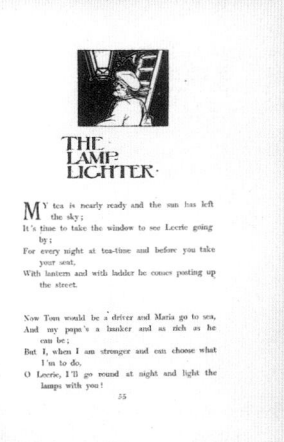

A well-known poem by Robert Louis Stevenson in *A Child's Garden of Verses*, 1896.

# January

15

16

17

18

19

20

21

Binding, inlaid with mother-of-pearl, and painted by Jessie M. King, the Scottish artist and book-illustrator, 1903.

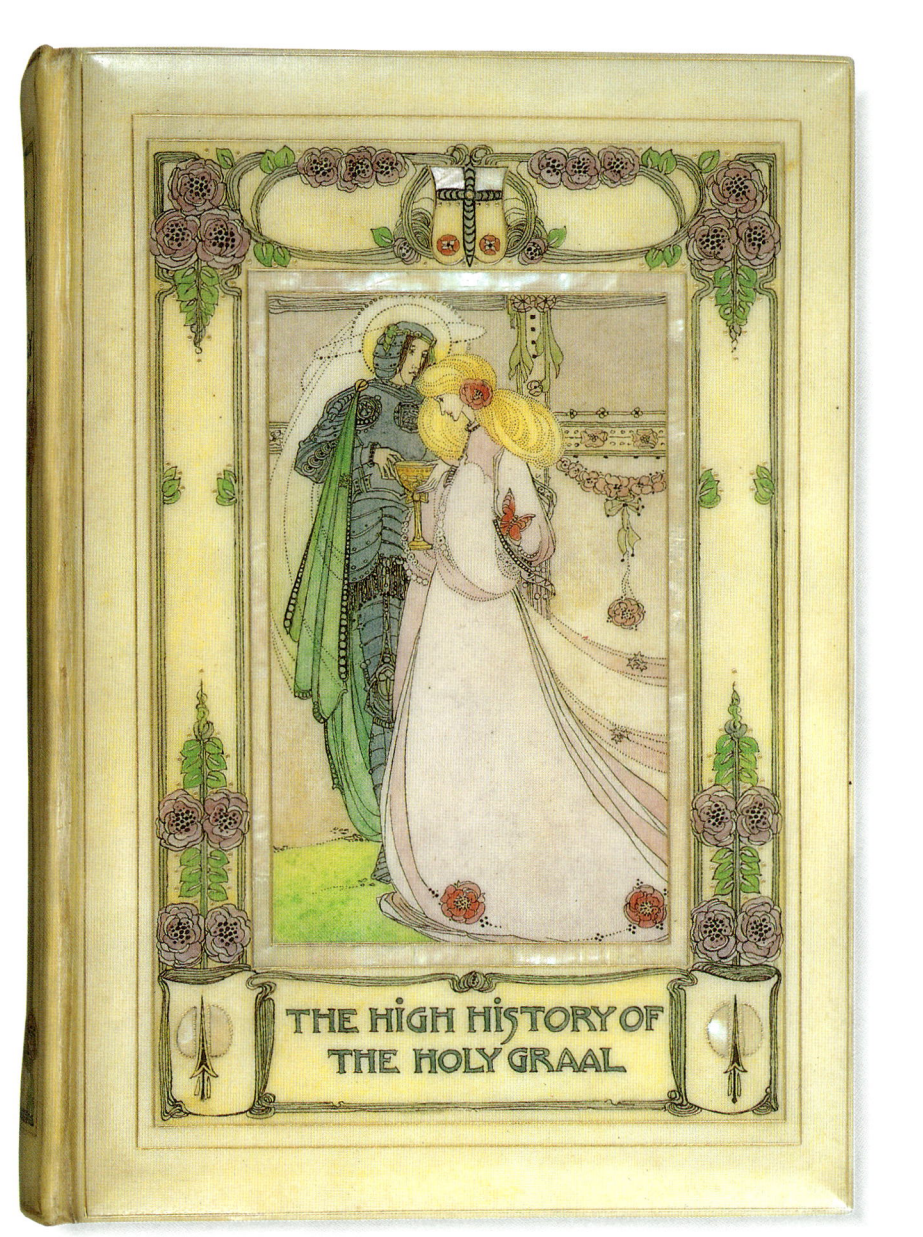

Had we never lov'd sae kindly,
Had we never lov'd sae blindly!
Never met — or never parted,
We had ne'er been broken-hearted. —

O Fare-thee-weel, thou first & fairest!
O Fare-thee-weel, thou best & dearest!
Thine be ilka joy & treasure,
Peace, Enjoyment, Love & Pleasure.
Ae fond kiss, & then we sever!
Ae fareweel, Alas, for ever!
Deep in heart-wrung tears I'll pledge thee,
Warring sighs & groans I'll wage thee. —

Song — To an old Scots tune —

Behold the hour, the boat, arrive!
My dearest Nancy, Oh, fareweel!
Sever'd frae thee can I survive
Frae thee wham I hae lov'd sae weel!

# January

22

23

24

25

26

27

28

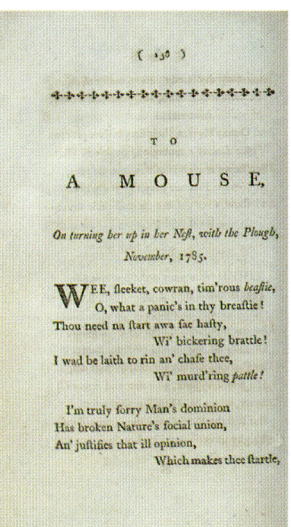

*Above.* A page of the rare 'Kilmarnock Burns', the first published collection of Burns's poems, 1786.

*Opposite.* The last verses of his poem, 'Ae Fond Kiss', written by Robert Burns in a letter to Agnes McLehose ('Clarinda'), 1791.

# January/
February

29

30

31

1

2

3

4

Details of shipping seen in the Mediterranean, by an Italian engraver, early 19th century

# February

5

6

7

8

9

10

11

# February

12

13

14

15

16

17

18

Design for a music room by Charles Rennie Mackintosh as part of his entry for an international competition in 1902.

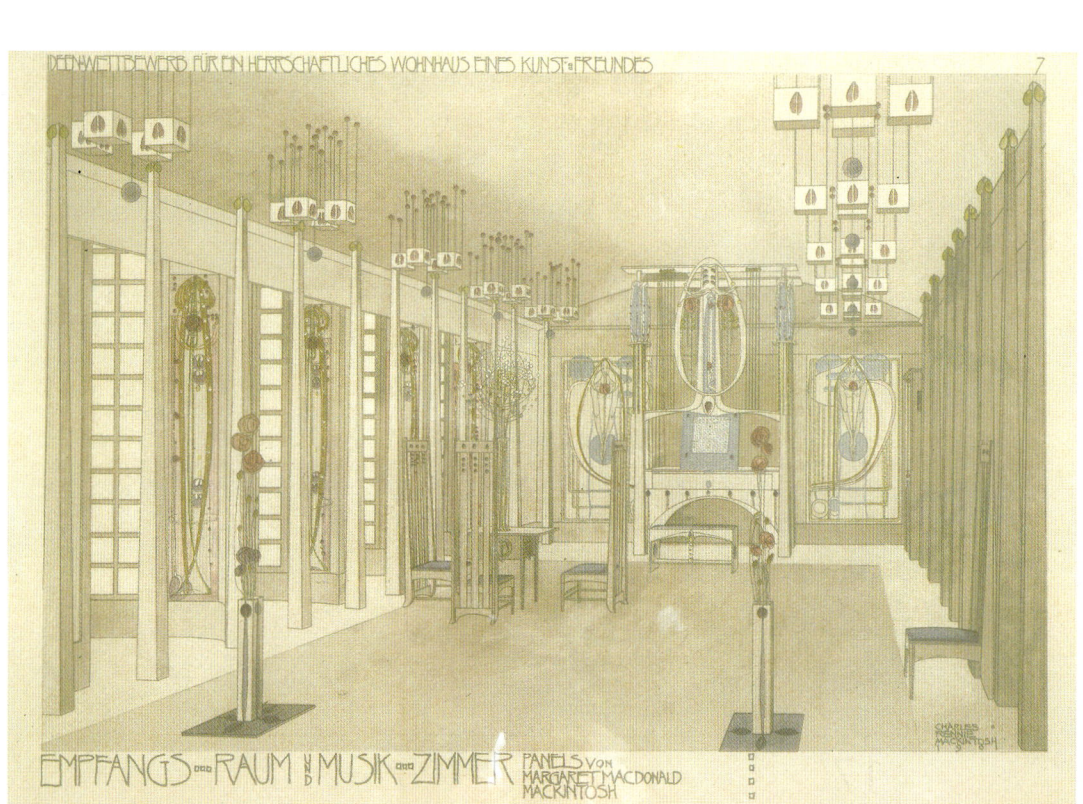

# February

19

20

21

22

23

24

25

*Above*. One of the author's adventures in Africa before he became a bishop, 1882.

*Opposite*. The author travelled for 90 days to meet her explorer husband at Lake Tanganyika in 1882.

benedicta dextera al-

ta ns icensi. Mag-
ño laudes
et per ho-
ficat. rascula. a.

Elisabeth

zacharie magnū uirū

FEBRUARY/
MARCH

26

27

28

29

1

2

3

Illuminated initials from an
Italian choirbook, c. 1460.

*Previous page*. Linlithgow Palace
in West Lothian, painted by a
Breton artist, Michel Bouquet, in
1849.

# March

4

5

6

7

8

9

10

Details from a Victorian scrap album.

# March

11

12

13

14

15

Wood-engravings, 1940–1, by the Scottish artist Agnes Miller Parker. Reproduced by permission of Mrs A. D. Quickenden.

16

17

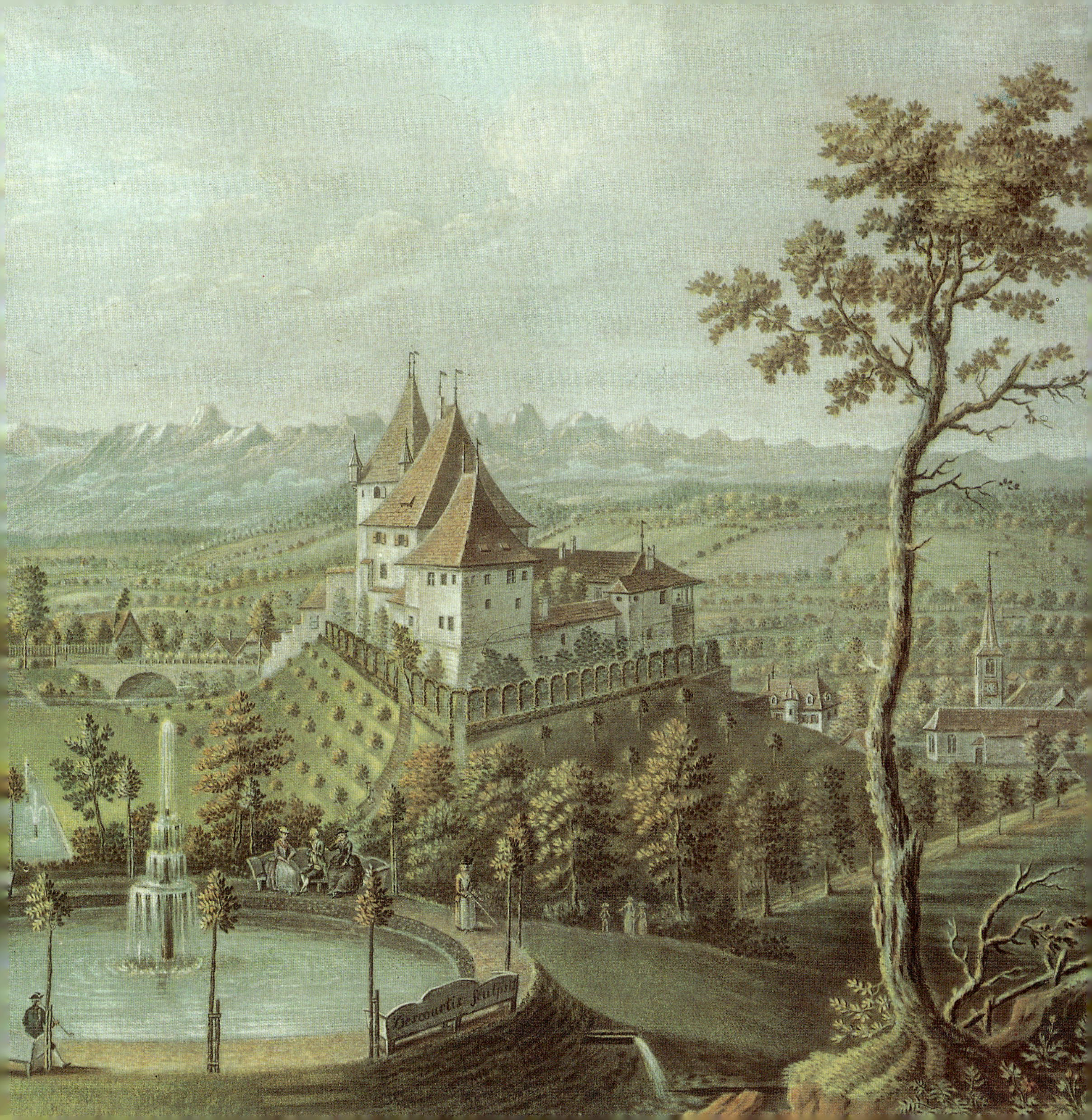
Descourtis Sculpsit

# March

18

19

20

21

22

23

24

A tiny manuscript prayerbook made in Padua in the 15th century; the Annunciation scene was added later.

*Previous page.* A view of the Alps from the Château de Worb near Berne, 1785.

INCIPIT OFFICI-
VM BEATSSIME
VIRGINIS MARIE
SECVDO SVET RO
MANE CVRIE V

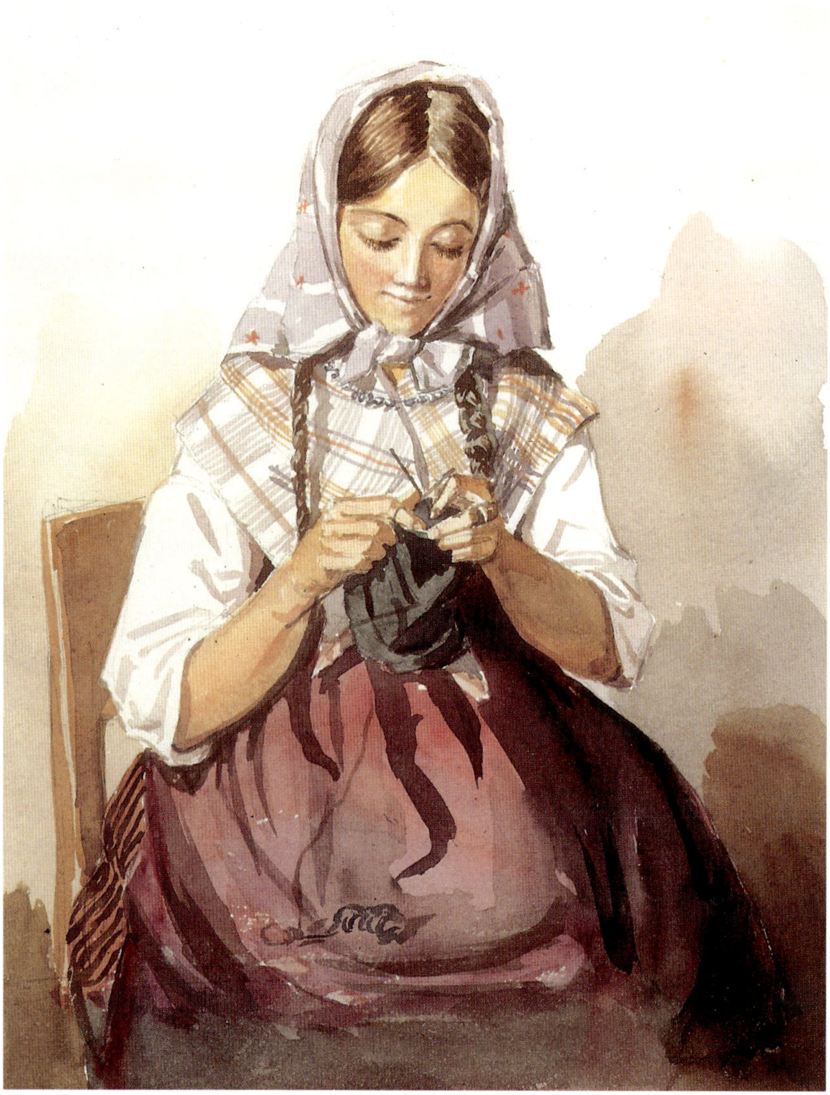

# MARCH

25

26

27

28

29

30

31

*Above.* Two varieties of gladiolus drawn by the artist on a single stem, 1842.

*Opposite.* The daughter of the parish clerk of Kvikkjock in Swedish Lappland, painted by John Francis Campbell of Islay, 1850.

# April

1

2

3

4

5

6

7

The Victorians believed in educational pastimes like this jigsaw puzzle of the map of Europe, made in 1908.

NEW DISSECTED MAPS
EUROPE.
INDIAN OCEAN
BLACK SEA
Sea of Azof
Sinope
Aleppo
EUROP
British Miles

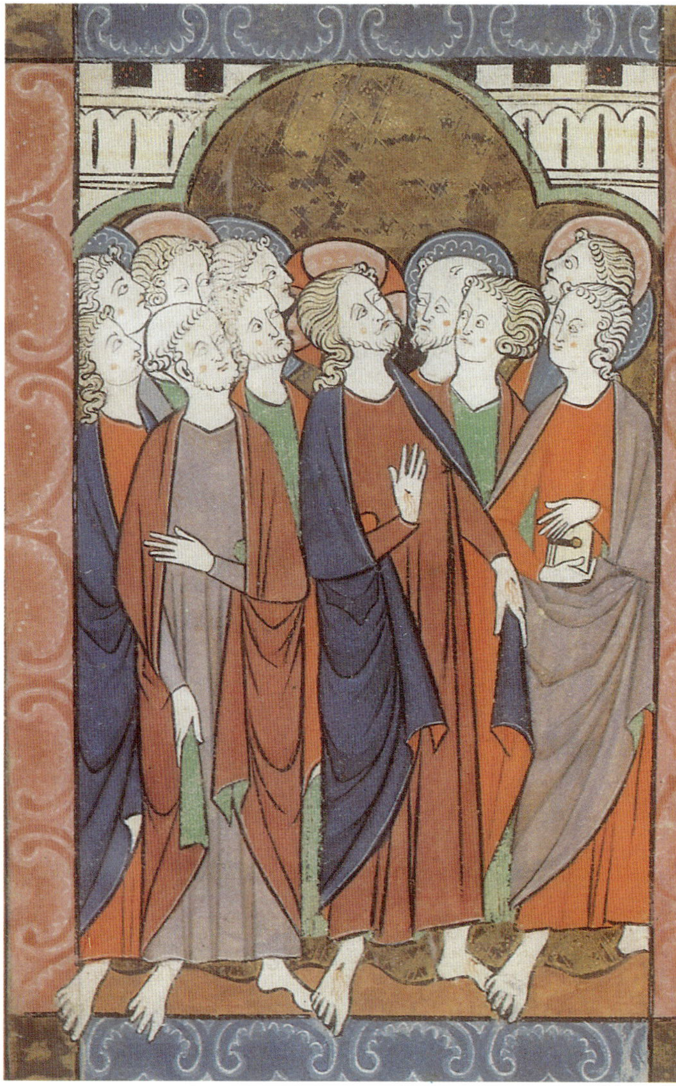

# April

8

9

10

11

12

13

14

Christ with the Apostles from an English prayerbook, late 13th century.

# April

15

16

17

18

19

20

21

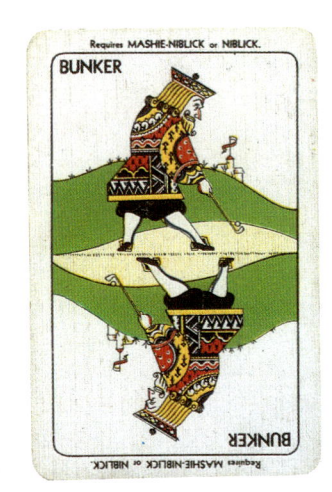

From a pack of cards intended for games of 'golf at the card table' in the 1930s.

Stroke negatived and TWO turns missed.
LOST BALL
DRIVE 220
Off Tee only.
Negatives ordinary PUTT.
MISSED PUTT
IRON 170
Requires MASHIE, MASHIE-NIBLICK or NIBLICK.
SLICED TO ROUGH

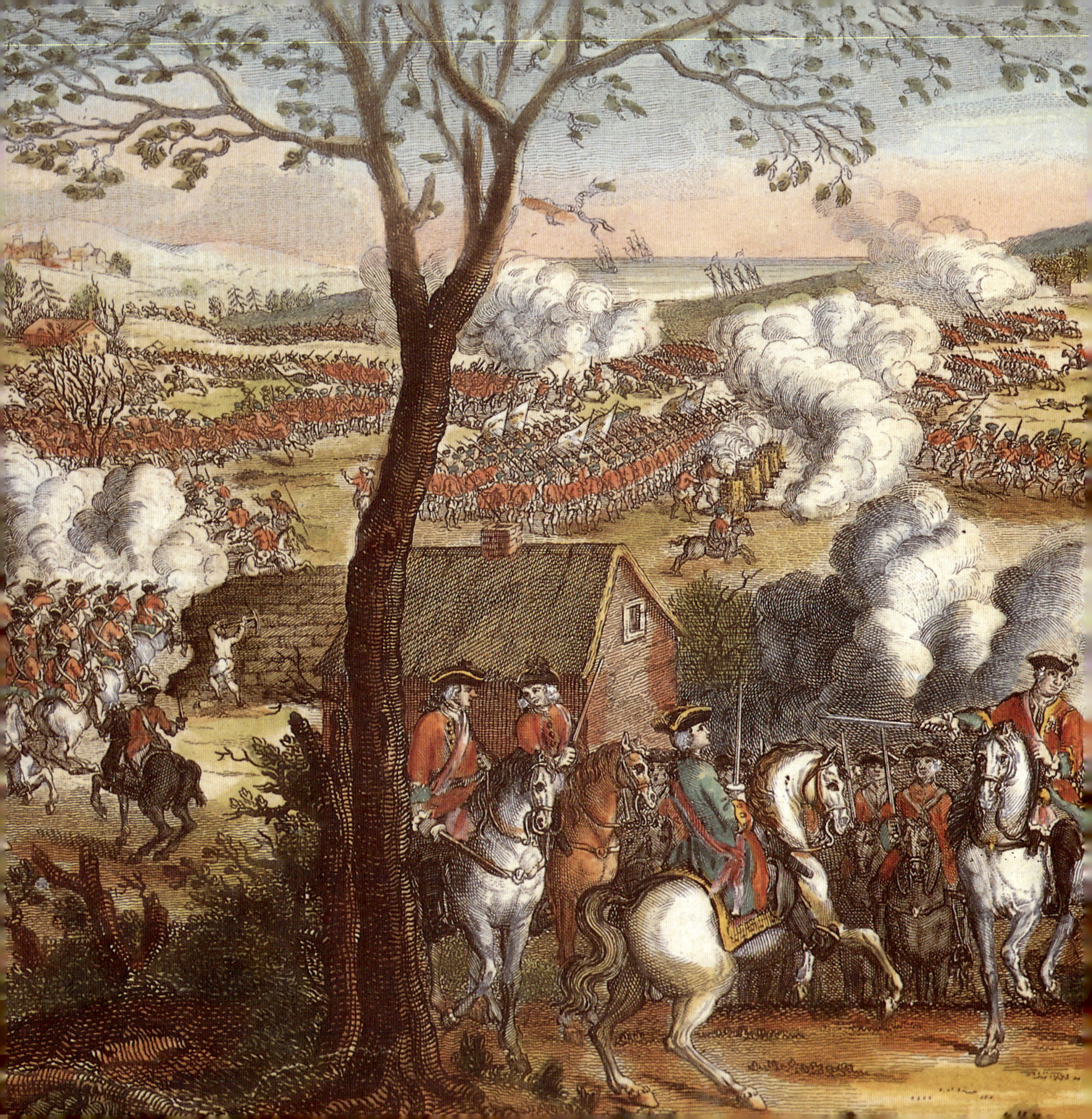

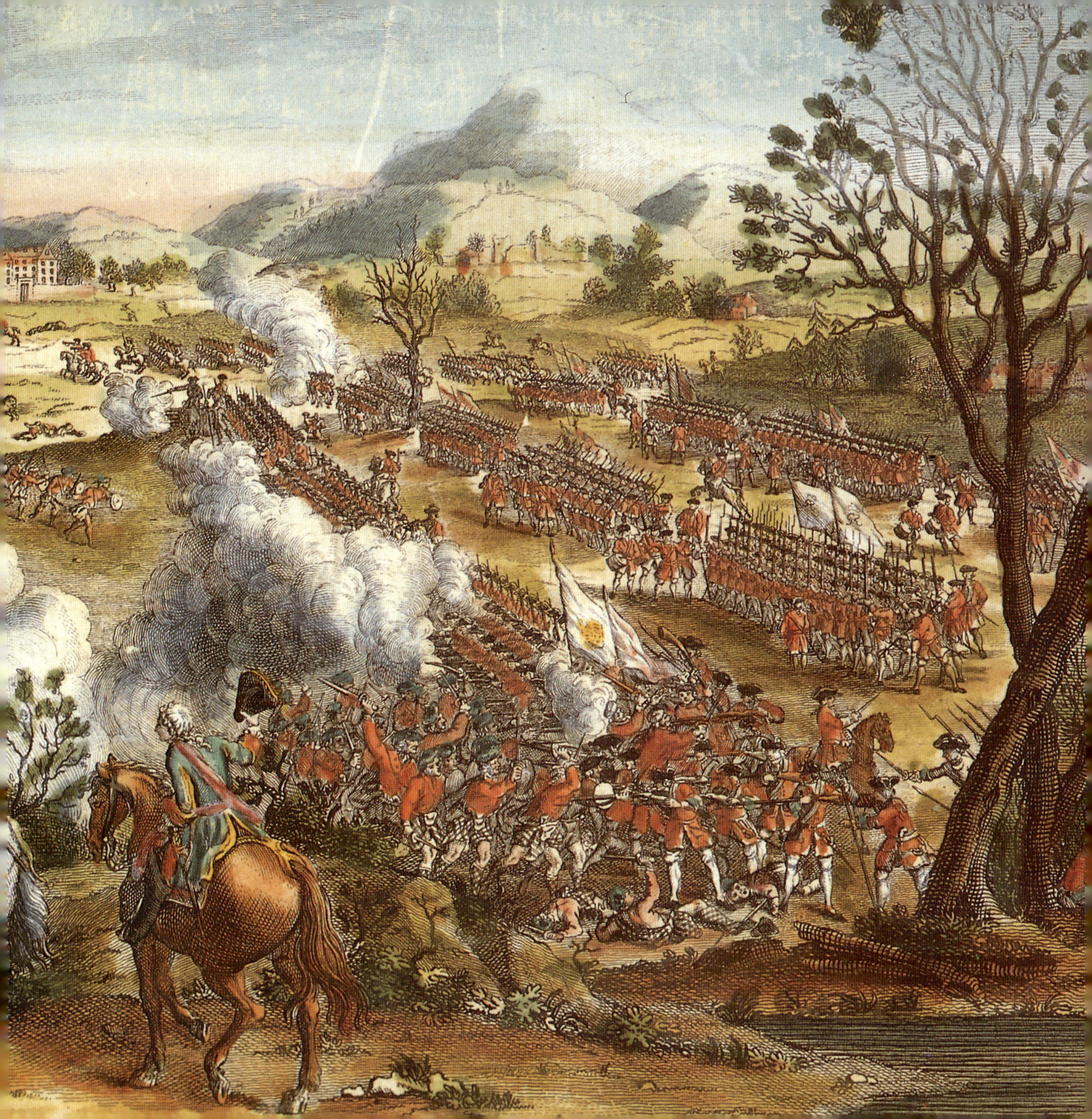

# April

22

23

24

25

26

27

28

*Previous page.* Hand-coloured engraving of the battle of Culloden, 1746.

APRIL/
MAY

29

30

1

2

3

4

5

Book-jacket designed by Jessie M. King, 1913.

# May

6

7

8

9

10

11

12

*Above*. Detail from the border of a printed Italian breviary of 1478.

*Opposite*. St Christopher carrying the Christ Child across a river, from a prayerbook made for a French lady, 15th century.

## Oratio de sancto Christofore. Antiphona.

**C**hristofore, pro salvatoris honore, fac
nos vros fore dignos deitatis amore.
promisso xpi quod petis obtinuisti. da populo tristi bona que moriendo petisti. confer solamen

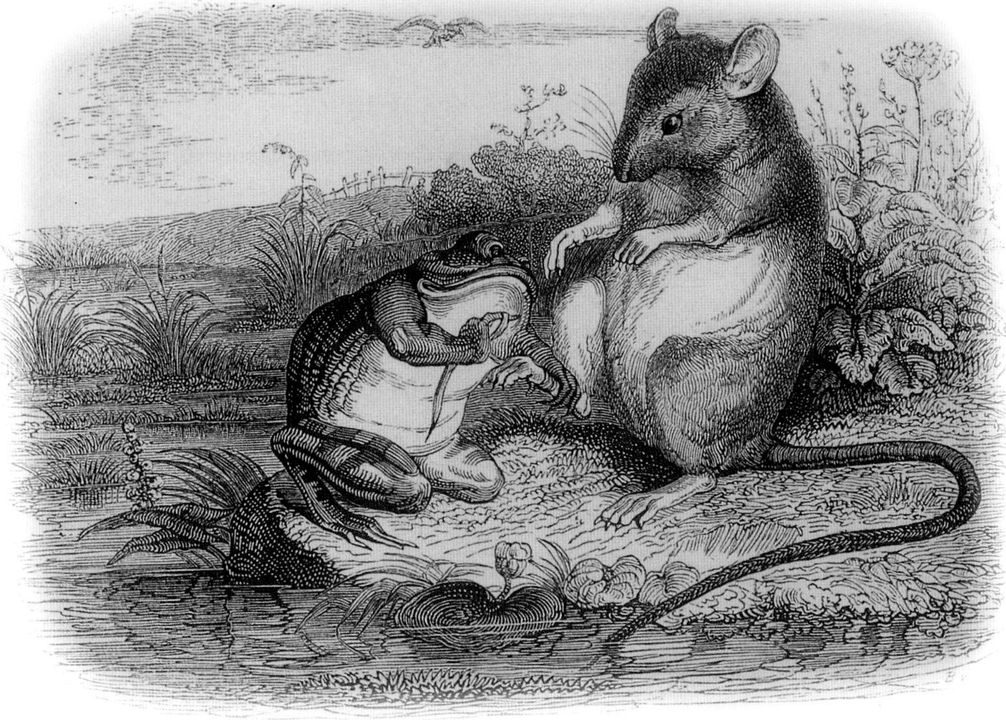

MAY

13

14

15

16

17

18

19

*Above.* Sketch by Walter Reid, a seal-engraver working in Edinburgh and Paris, c. 1860–70.

*Opposite.* The fable of the frog who tried to drown the rat, illustrated by the French artist Jean Grandville, 1838.

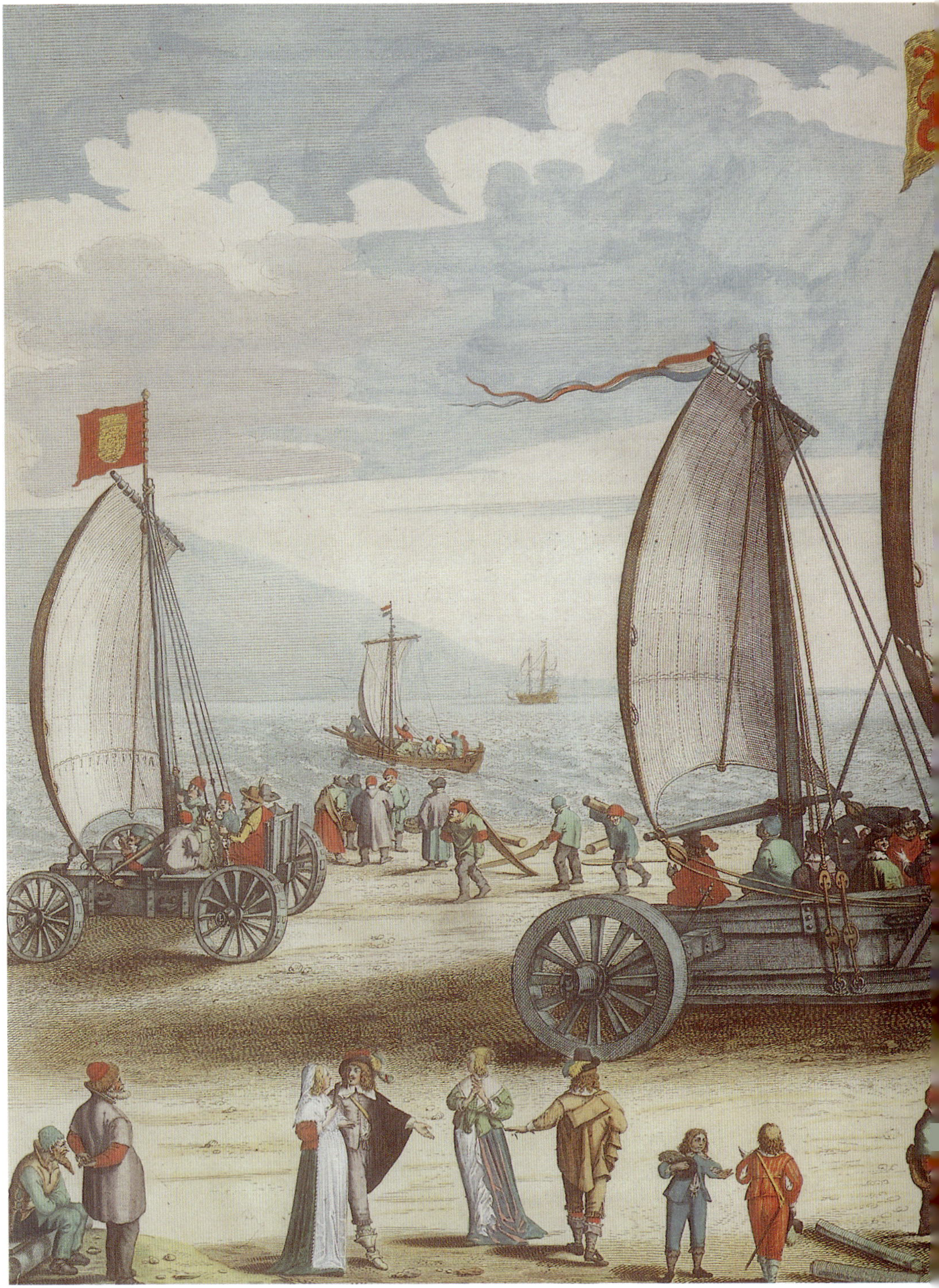

The 'Veli-voli currus', a wheeled boat built for Prince Maurice of Nassau, 1649. Reproduced by permission of Mr John Bartholomew.

# May

20

21

22

23

24

25

26

*Above.* Scottish costume for an entertainment at the Bavarian court in 1835.

*Opposite.* A fine example of a Scottish binding of the first half of the 18th century.

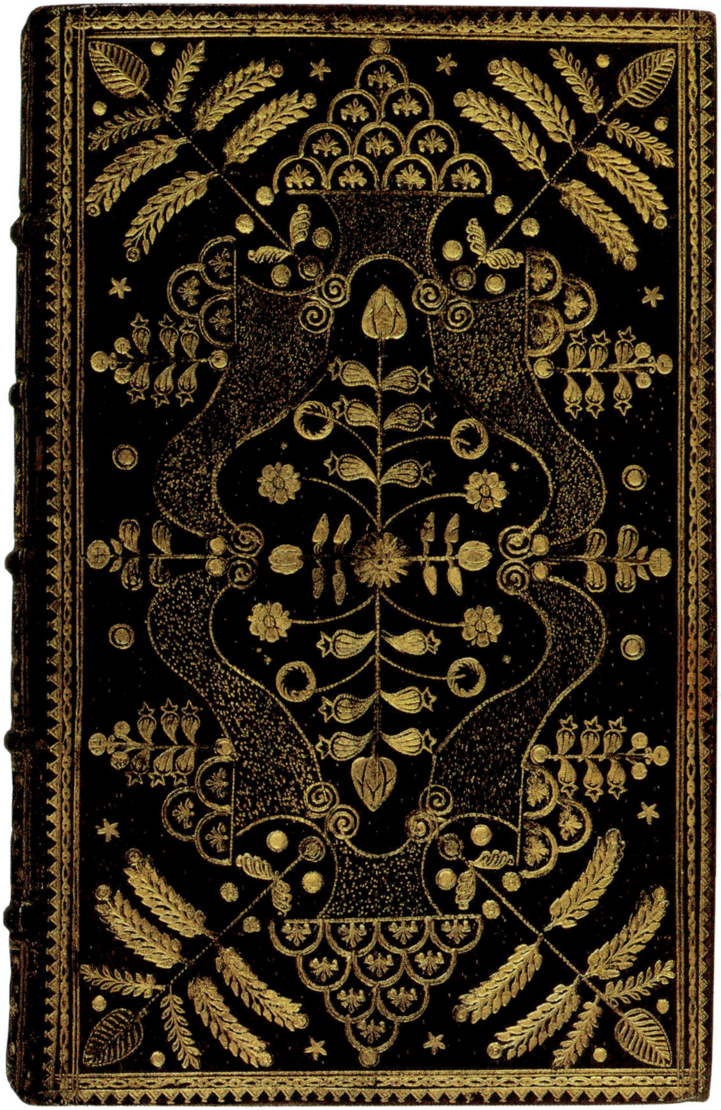

# May/
# June

27

28

29

30

31

1

2

An Italian cardinal, one of a series of figures painted in Padua and Venice, late 16th century.

JUNE

3

4

5

6

7

8

9

Skilled writing-masters took pride in their ability to draw a figure with a continuous stroke of the pen, as in this Portuguese example of 1722.

# June

10

11

12

13

14

15

16

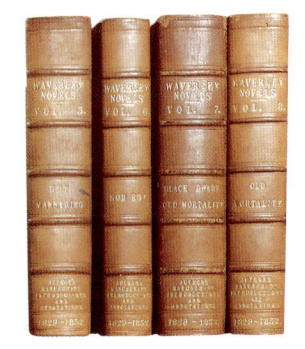

*Above.* Part of the 'Magnum Opus', the interleaved set of the Waverley Novels made specially for Sir Walter Scott, which he used to correct and revise his work for the Magnum Edition of 1829–33.

*Opposite.* Washerwomen on the Calton Hill, Edinburgh, 1825.

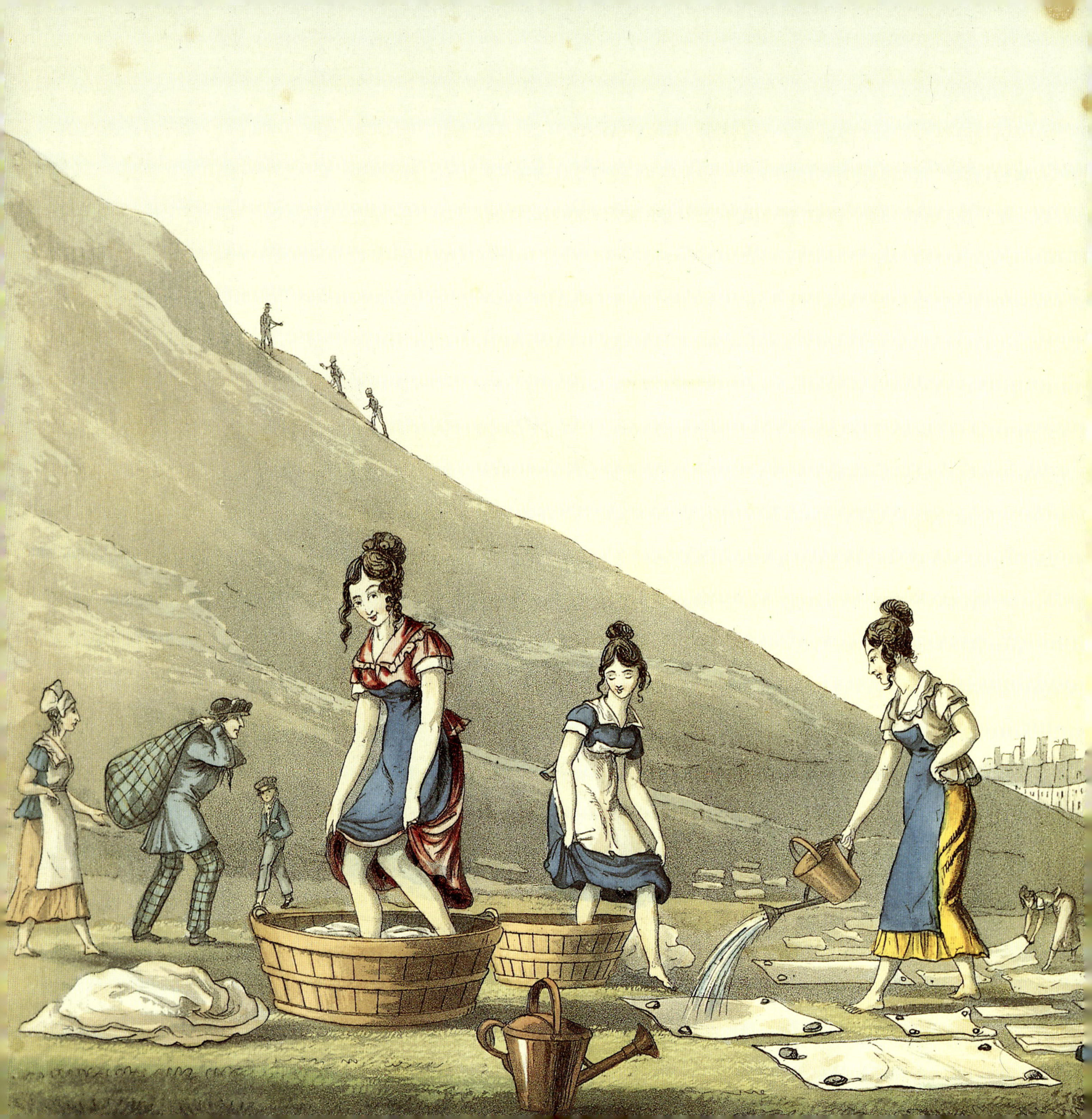

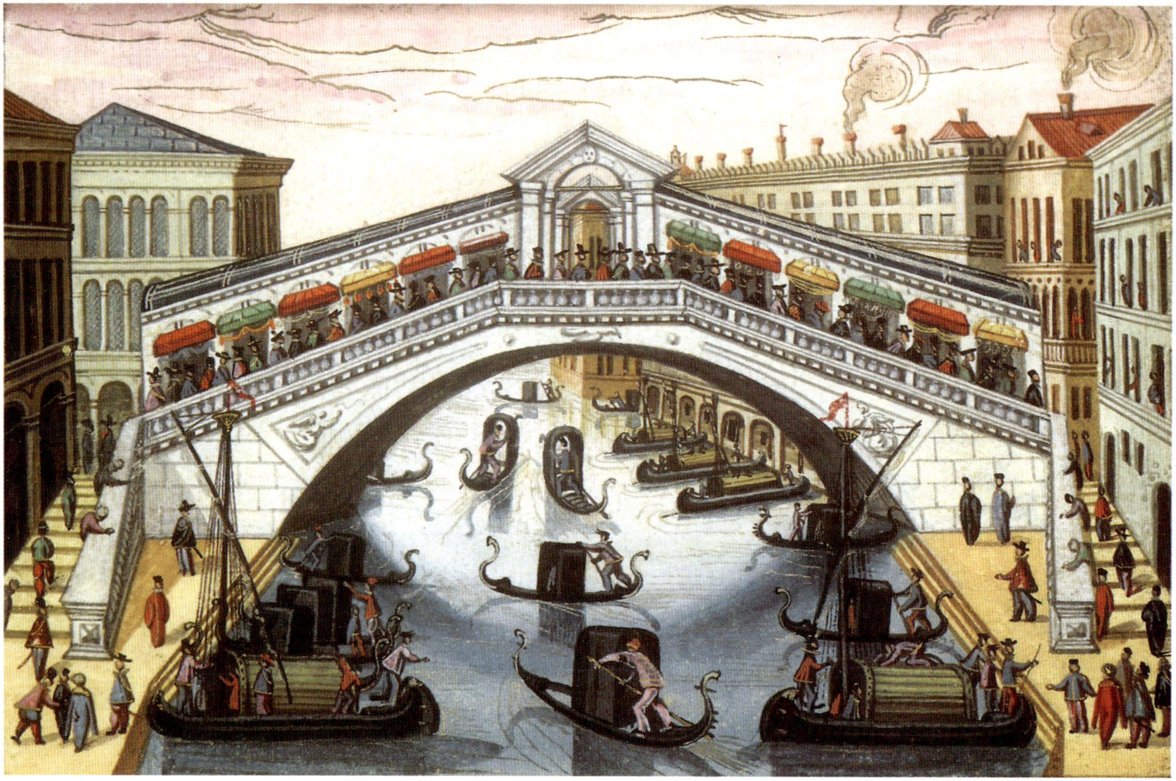

# June

17

18

19

20

21

22

23

The Rialto Bridge in Venice, and (above) Venetian masked figures, late 16th century.

# June

24

25

26

27

28

29

30

# July

1

2

3

4

5

6

7

Some of the attractive covers of tourist maps first published by the Ordnance Survey in the 1920s.

# July

8

9

10

11

12

13

14

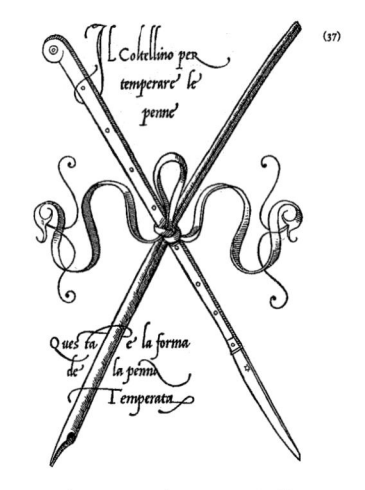

*Above.* A 16th-century Italian writing-master's tools.

*Opposite.* St Luke, painted in the style of the French artist Jean Bourdichon, c. 1500.

N ILLO·TĒPORE·MISSVS·EST·ANGELVS·GABRI

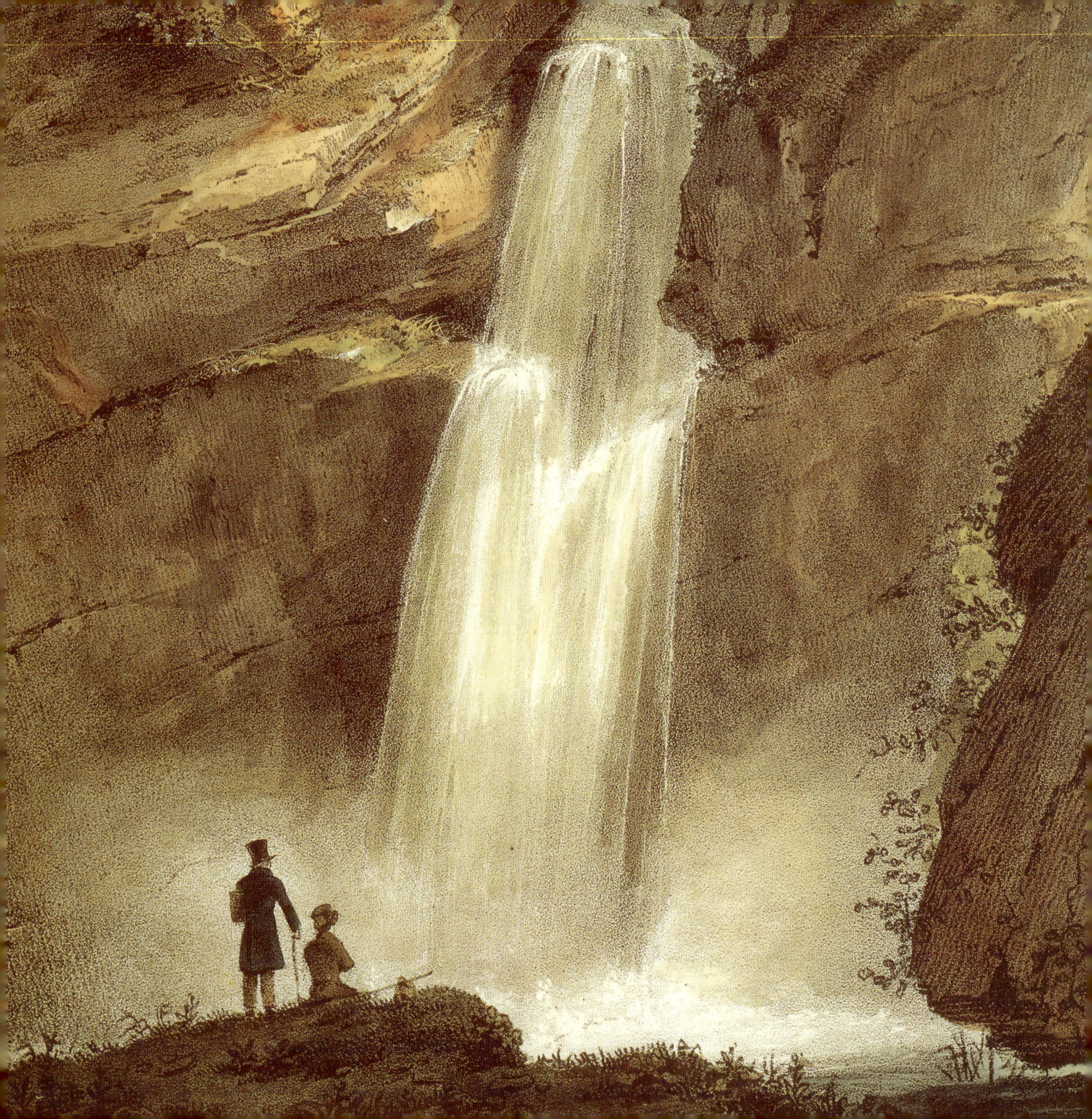

JULY

15

16

17

18

19

20

21

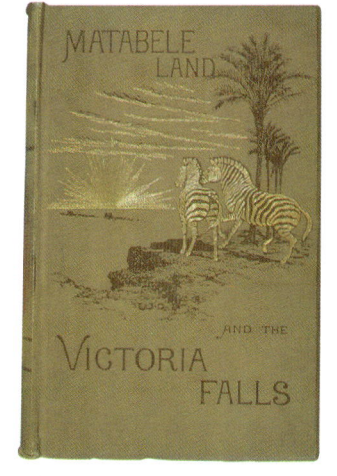

*Above.* A book-binder's view of Africa, 1889.

*Opposite.* The lower fall of Foyers, Inverness-shire, 1825.

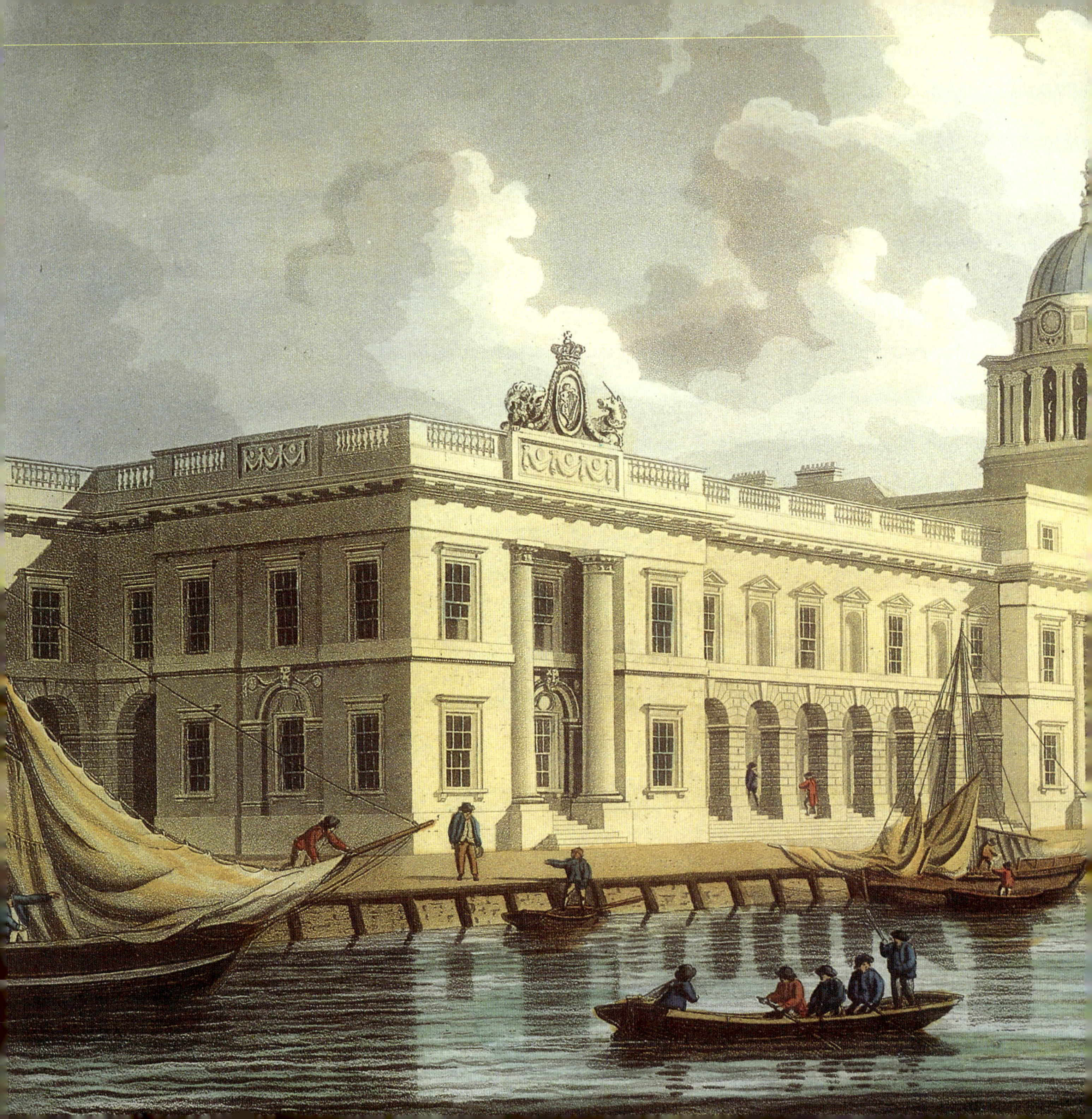

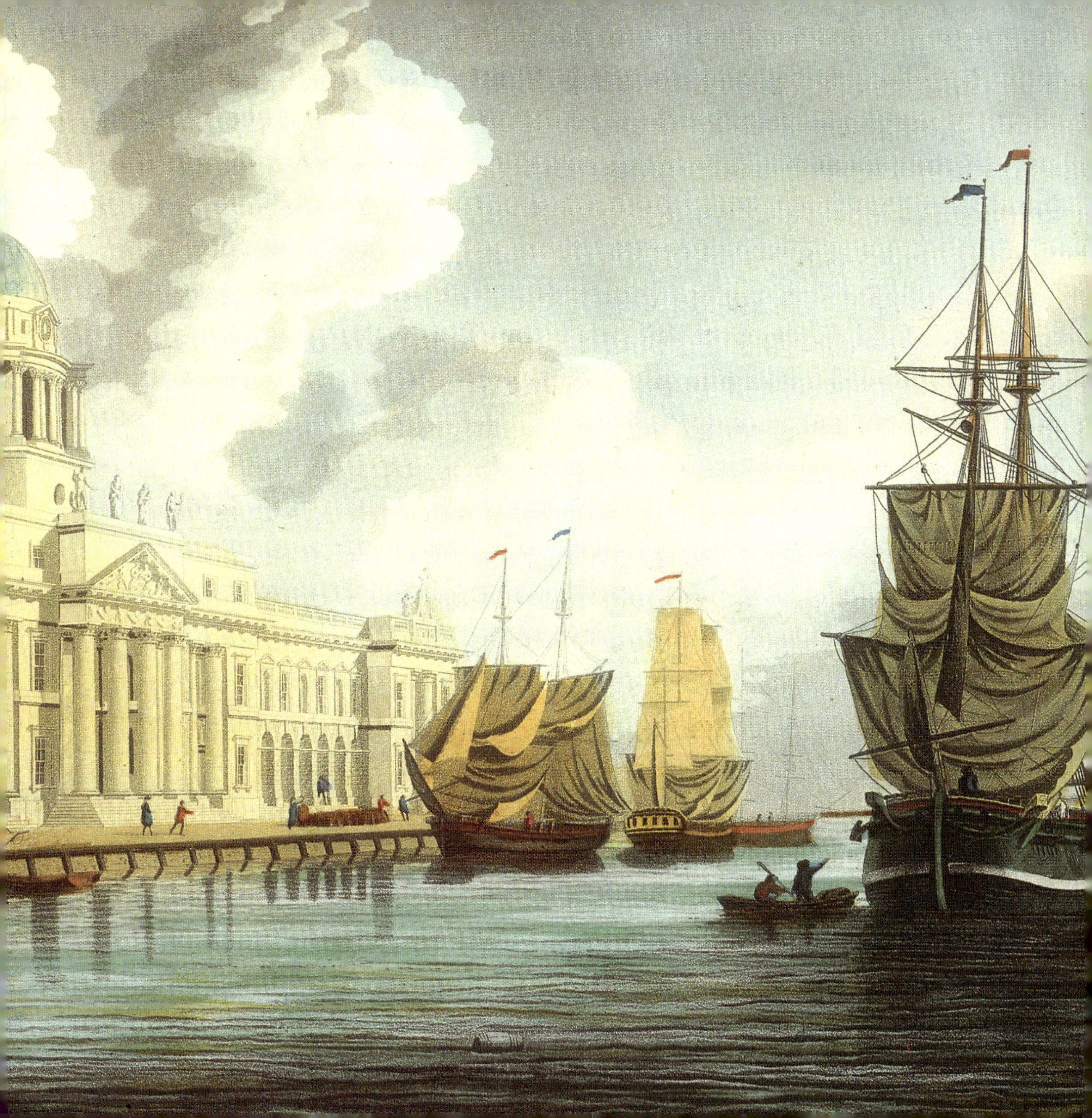

# July

22

23

24

25

26

27

28

Pen-drawings by the seal-engraver, Walter Reid, c. 1860–70.

*Previous page*. An early 19th-century view of the Custom House, Dublin, by James Malton.

July/
August

29

30

31

1

2

3

4

AUGUST

5

6

7

8

9

10

11

**cuileag**

The only known copy of a Gaelic grammar for schoolchildren, printed in the 1870s.

## LEASANAN.

cat   cearc   muc

cù   cùdainn   cuileag

[THOIR FAINEAR.—Leugh na focail do 'n leanabh; an sin thoir air an leanabh an leughadh gus am bi e min-eolach orra. Tha mearachdan gun chrìch, agus eas-ordugh ag èirigh o bhi 'dearmad na steidh shimplidh, gum bu chòir am focal bhi air a *leughadh* an toiseach, agus air a *litreachadh* a rìs. NA IARR GU BRÀTH AIR LEANABH FOCAL AIR BITH A LITREACHADH GUS AN ABAIR E AN TOISEACH E GU PONGAIL.]

### LEASAN.

cù, cat, cearc, muc, cùdainn, cuileag.

Cù agus cat.

Cearc agus cuileag.

Muc agus cùdainn.

## READING-LESSONS.

cat   hen   pig

dog   tub   fly

[NOTE.—Read these words to the child; then make the child read them till it is perfectly familiar with them. Endless mistakes and confusion arise from overlooking the simple principle that the *reading* of a word should come first, and the *spelling* of it afterwards. NEVER ASK A CHILD TO SPELL ANY WORD TILL IT HAS PRONOUNCED IT.]

### EXERCISE.

dog, cat, hen, pig, tub, fly.

A dog and a cat.

A hen and a fly.

A pig and a tub.

Prima ego velivolis ambivi cursibus Orbem,
Magellane novo te duce ducta freto.
Ambivi, meritoq3 vocor VICTORIA: sunt mi
Vela, alæ; precium, gloria; pugna, mare.

# August

12

13

14

15

16

17

18

*Above.* Engraving of an armillary sphere, used in astronomy to represent the heavens, 1665.

*Opposite.* Detail from a map of the Pacific Ocean by the great Flemish mapmaker, Abraham Ortelius, 1592.

# August

19

20

21

22

23

24

25

The cover of a Victorian song-sheet, 1879.

# "THE CATS' AT HOME."

**SONG**

WRITTEN BY **G. F. W.**

THE MUSIC COMPOSED BY **H. P. DANKS.**

LONDON ROBERT COCKS & Co NEW BURLINGTON STREET, REGENT STREET
BY SPECIAL APPOINTMENT

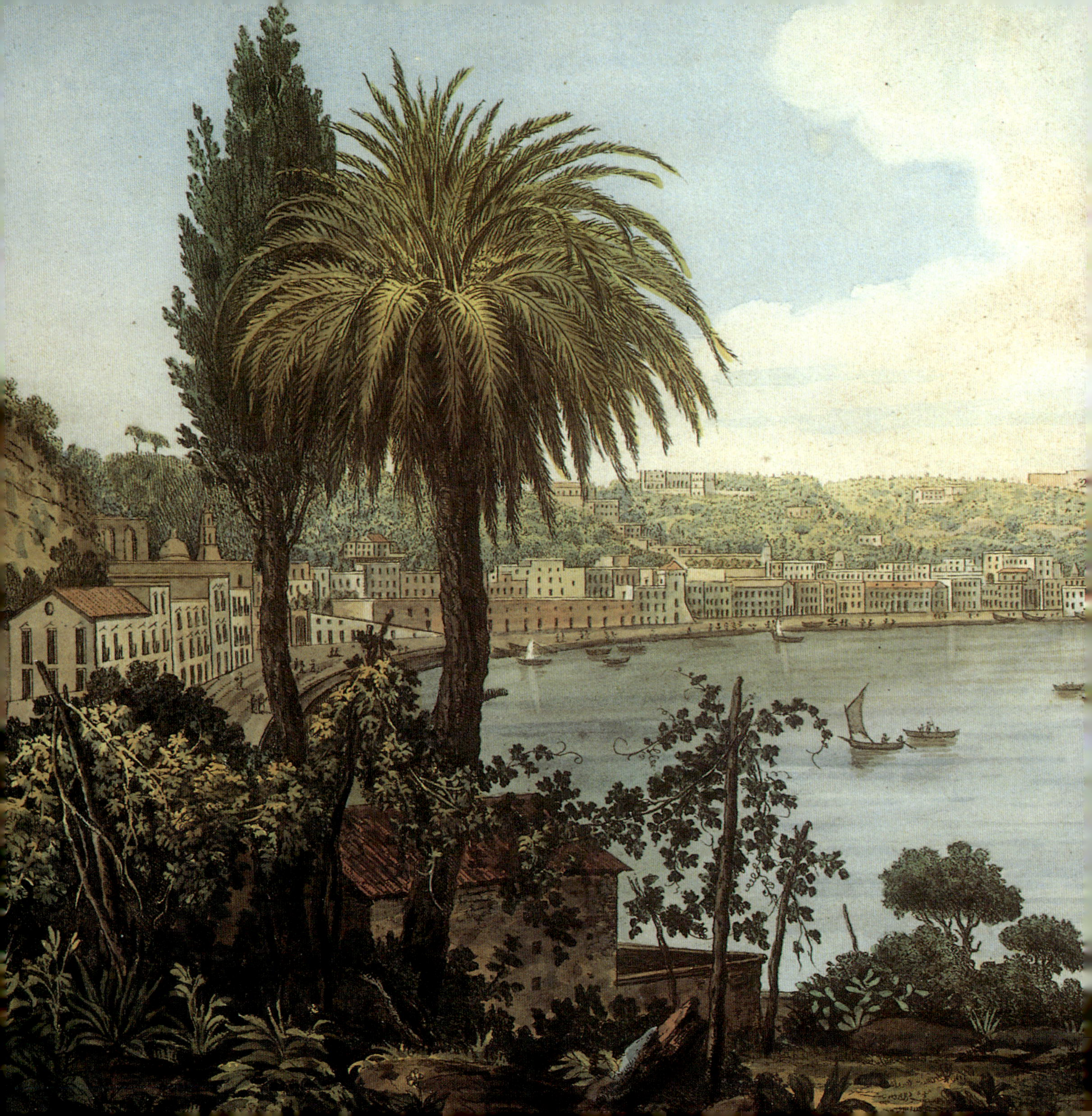

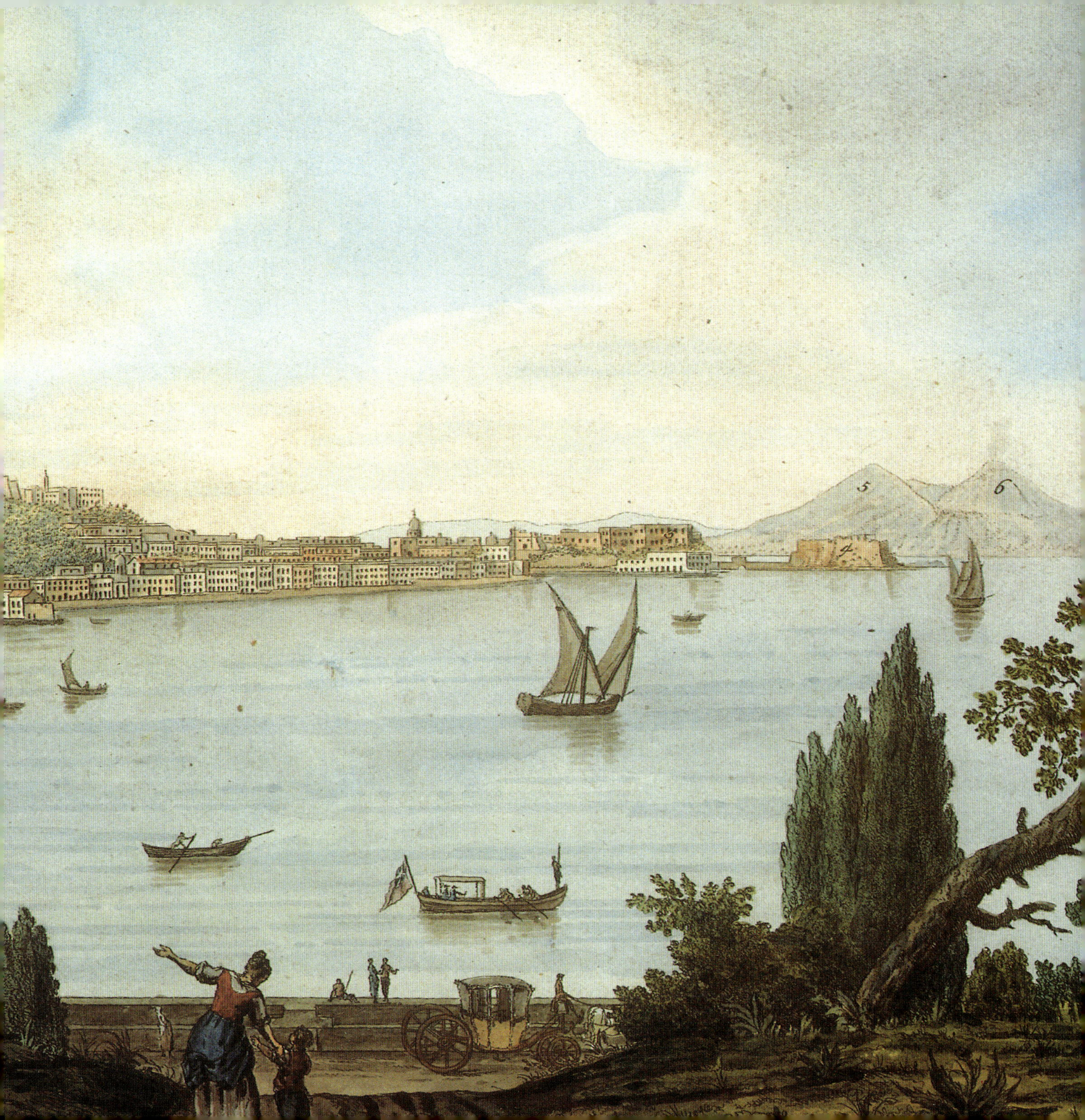
5
6
4

# August/ September

26

27

28

29

30

31

1

*Opposite.* The Mughal Emperor Aurungzeb watching a fight between a lion and an elephant, c. 1820.

*Previous page.* View of Naples from Pausilippo in Sir William Hamilton's work on Italian volcanoes, 1776.

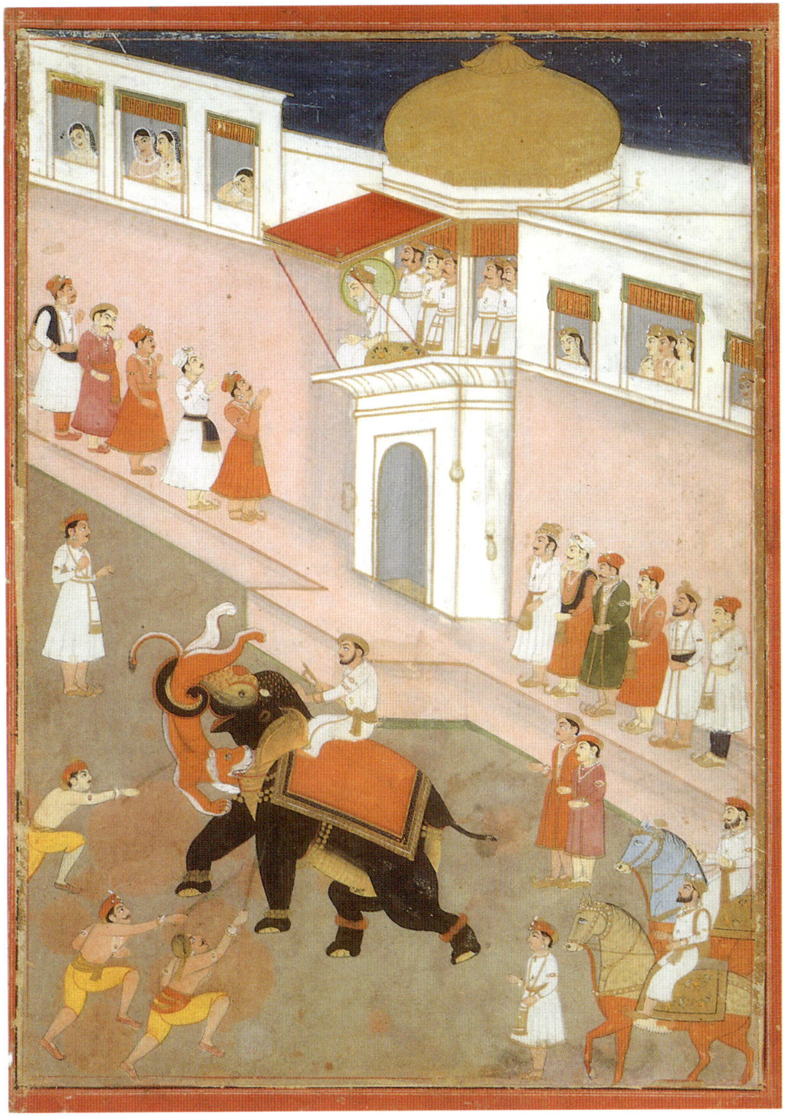

# September

2

3

4

5

6

7

8

Different kinds of North American kinglets, a bird related to the European goldcrest, 1835.

SEPTEMBER

9

10

11

12

13

14

15

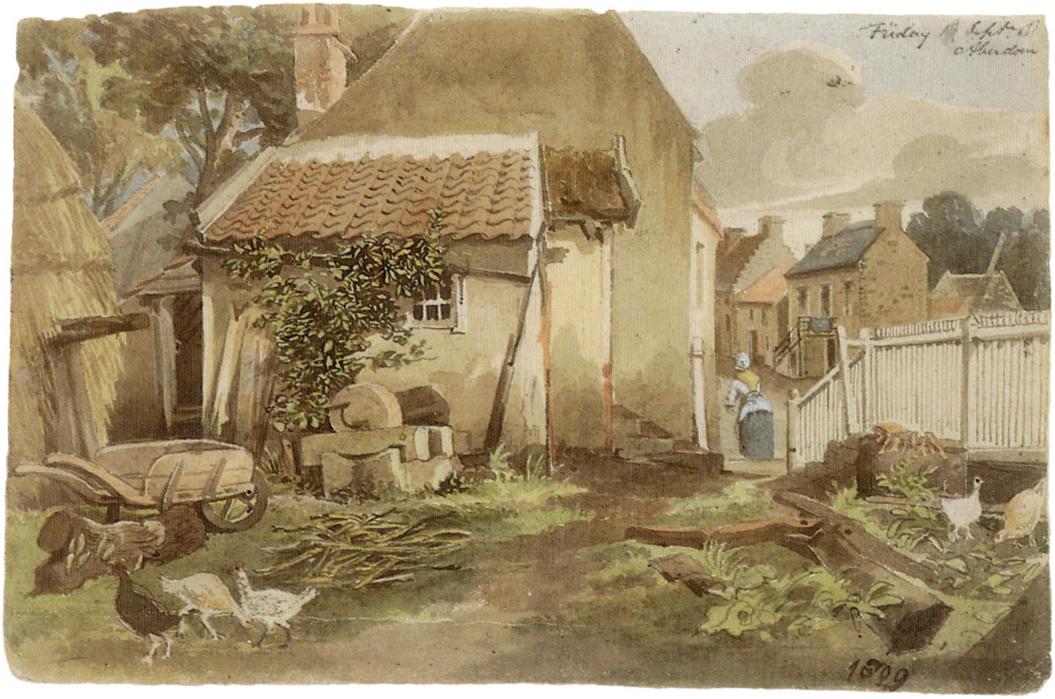
Friday
1809

# September

16

17

18

19

20

21

22

Watercolour of Aberdour, Fife, by John Harden, an accomplished amateur painter, 1809.

# September

23

24

25

26

27

28

29

Two North American jays and a magpie, 1835.

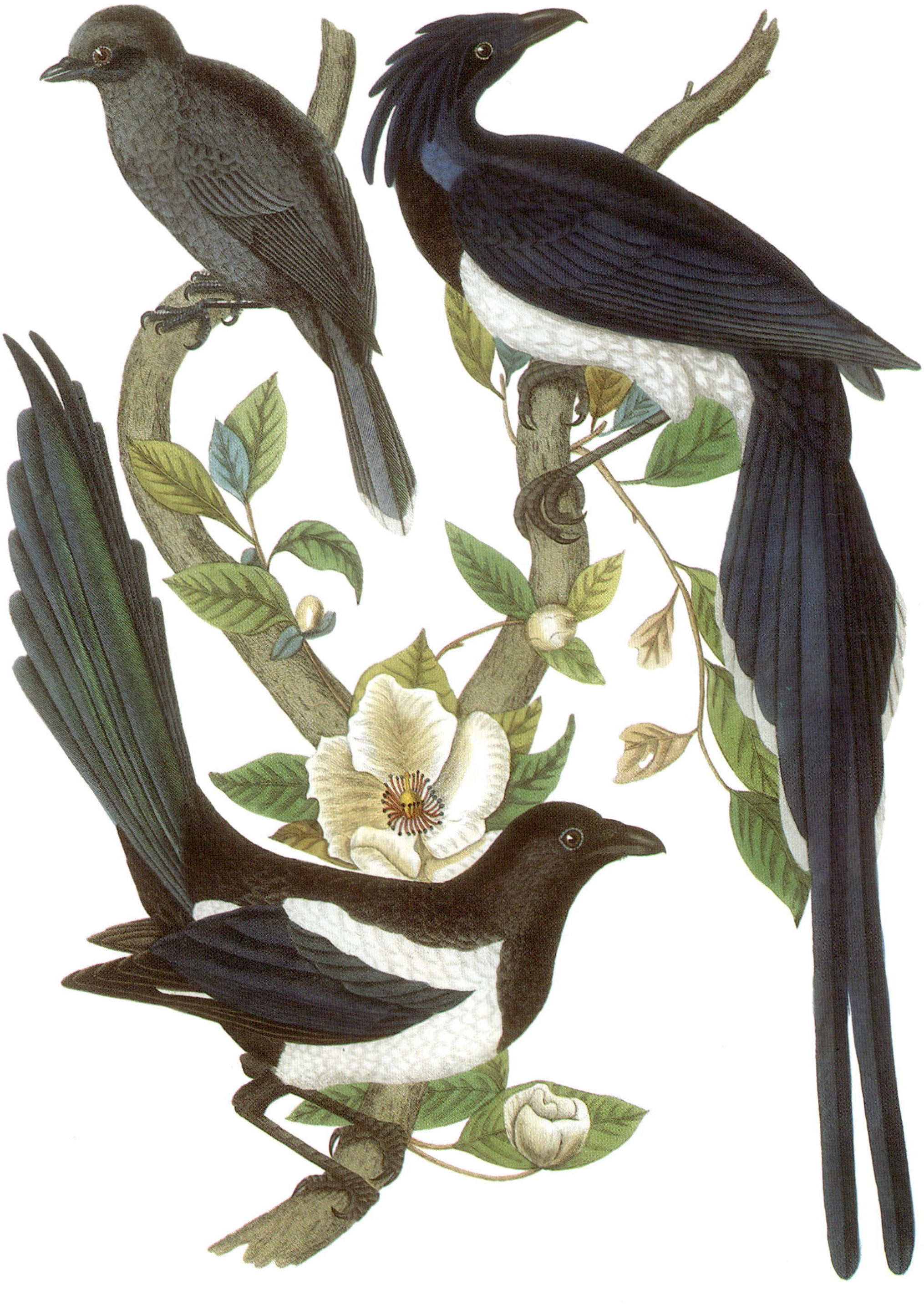

# THE INTERNATIONAL STRUGGLE
### BETWEEN
## ENGLAND, SCOTLAND, IRELAND, FRANCE & AMERICA
### 48 HOURS' WORLD'S CHAMPIONSHIP!
## £100 PRIZES and TROPHY.

## WAVERLY MARKET, EDINBURGH
October 24th to 29th, 1887, at 2-30 to 10-30 Daily.

## RALPH TEMPLE & W. S. MALTBY
**AMERICA.**     **AUSTRALIA.**

Champion Trick and Unicycle Riders, Perform Afternoon and Evening.    BAND IN ATTENDANCE.

Short Races Each Night.     **Admission, 6d.**

SEPTEMBER/
OCTOBER

30

1

2

3

4

5

6

Poster for an international
bicycle race in Edinburgh, 1887.

# October

7

8

9

10

11

12

13

James V and his first wife, Madeleine of France, from a 16th-century Scottish heraldic manuscript.

OCTOBER

14

15

16

17

18

19

20

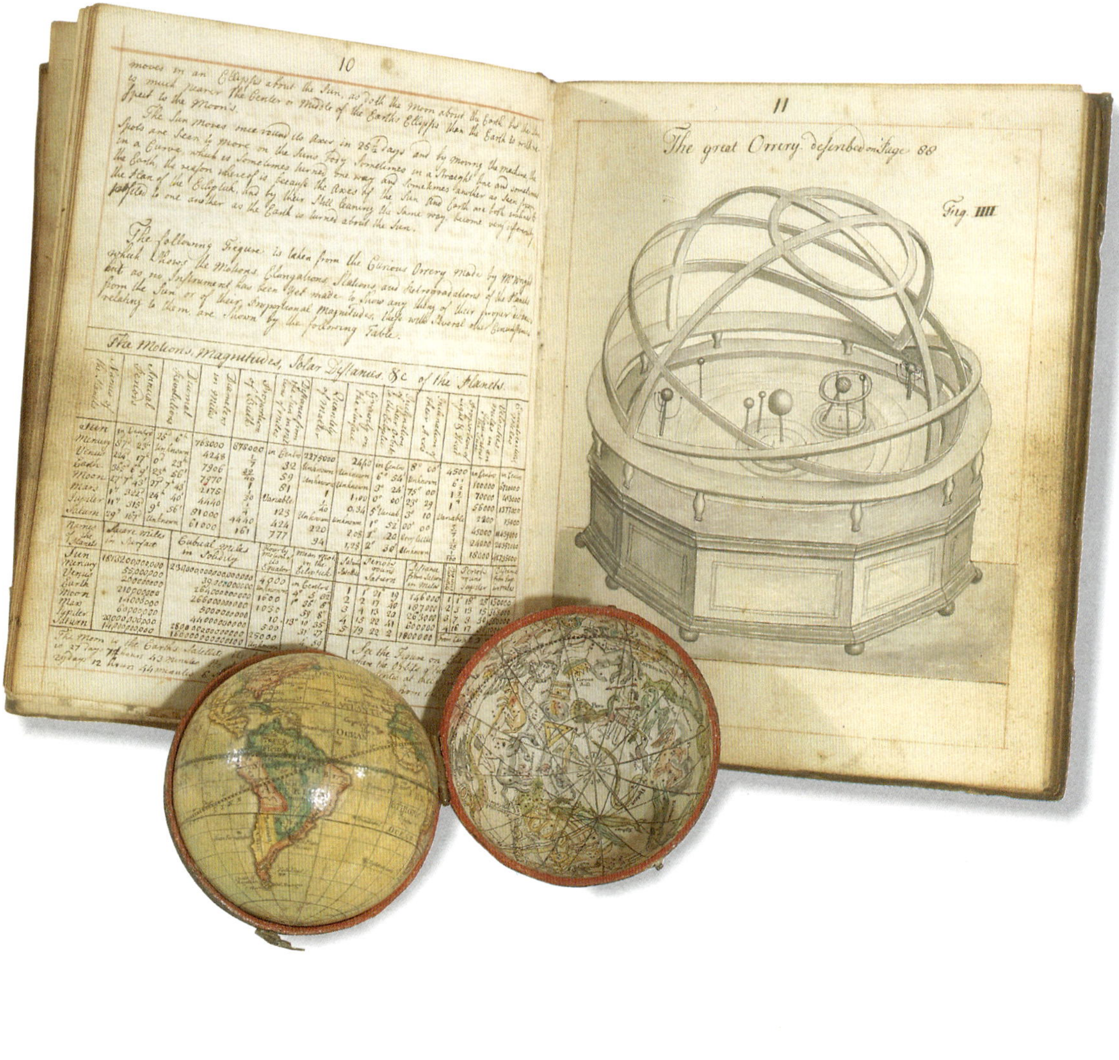
10
11
The great Orrery described in Page 88
Fig. IIII

# October

21

22

23

24

25

26

27

*Above.* A typical Scottish binding, known as a 'wheel' binding, on a legal thesis of 1774.

*Opposite.* A notebook with designs for instruments, and a pocket globe made by the 18th-century astronomer James Ferguson.

# October/
# November

28

29

30

31

1

2

3

Scotland from a volume of caricatures depicting the different countries of Europe, drawn in map form, 1869.

# SCOTLAND.

A gallant piper, struggling through the bogs,
His wind bag broken, wearing his clay clogs;

Yet, strong of heart, a fitting emblem makes
For Scotland—land of heroes and of cakes.

# November

4

5

6

7

8

9

10

Winter and spring fashions from a French ladies' magazine, 1787–8.

November

11

12

13

14

15

16

17

# Leo Belgicus

# November

18

19

20

21

22

23

24

*Above.* Figures from a Dutch engraving of 1649. Reproduced by permission of Mr John Bartholomew.

*Opposite.* An unusual representation of the seventeen Provinces which constituted the Netherlands towards the end of the 16th century.

November/
December

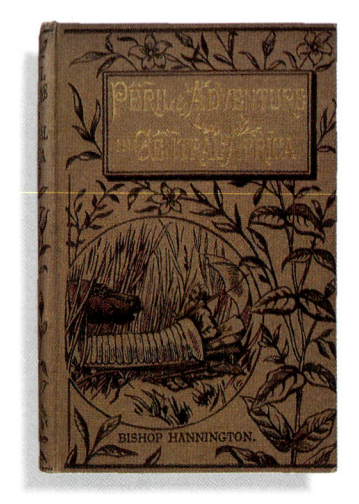

25

26

27

28

29

30

1

An unexpected awakening, 1886.

# December

2

3

4

5

6

7

8

Incident on a journey through Abyssinia in 1873.

proteste de la recepvoir innocente de tous crimes
quant je serois leur subiecte la religion catholique
& le mayntien du droit que dieu ma donné à
ceste couronne sont les deulx poincts de ma
condampnation & toutesfoys ilz ne me veullent
permettre de dire que cest pour la religion catolique
que je meurs mays pour la crainte du chaumgem[en]t
de la leur & pour preuve ilz mont osté mon
aulmonier lequel bien quil soit en la mayson Je
nay peu obtenir quil me vinst confesser ny
communier a ma mort mays mont faict grande
instance de recepvoir la consolation & doctrine
de leur ministre ammené pour ce faict ce porteur
& sa compaignie la pluspart de vos subiectz
vous tesmoigneront mes desportementz en ce
mien acte dernier il reste que je vous suplie
comme Roy tres chrestien mon beau frere & ancien
allyé & qui mavez tousiours protesté de
maymer qua ce coup vous fuysiez preuve en
toulz ces poincts de vostre vertu tant par
charité me soulageant de ce que pour descharger ma consscience je ne puis sans vous qui
est de recompenser mes serviteurs desolez leur

laysant leurs guges lauctre faysant pour dieu
pour une d'orne qui a esté nommee tres chrestienne
et meurt chatolique desnuee de toutz ses biens
quant a mon filz ie le vous recommande autant
qu'il le meritera car ie n'en puis respondre
Iay pris la hardiesse de vous envoier deulx
pierres rares pour la sante vous la desirant
parfaicte aueec heureuse et longue vie vous les
receuerez comme de vostre tres affectionnee
belle soeur mourante en vous rendant tesmoignage
de son bon cueur enuers vous ie vous recommande
encore mes serviteurs vous ordonnerez si il vous
plaict que pour mon ame ie soye payee de
partye de ce que me debuez et qu'en l'honneur
de Jhesus Christ lequel ie priray demayn a
ma mort pour vous me laisser de quoy fonder
un obit et fayre les aumosnes requises
ce mercredy a deulx heures apres minuit

Vostre tres affectionnee et bien
bonne soeur    Marie

A portrait of Mary by a French engraver.

The last letter of Mary, Queen of Scots, written on the eve of her execution in 1587, protesting her innocence and asking her brother-in-law to care for her servants.

## December

9

10

11

12

13

14

15

An engraving of Italian strolling musicians, c. 1827.

December

16

17

18

19

20

21

22

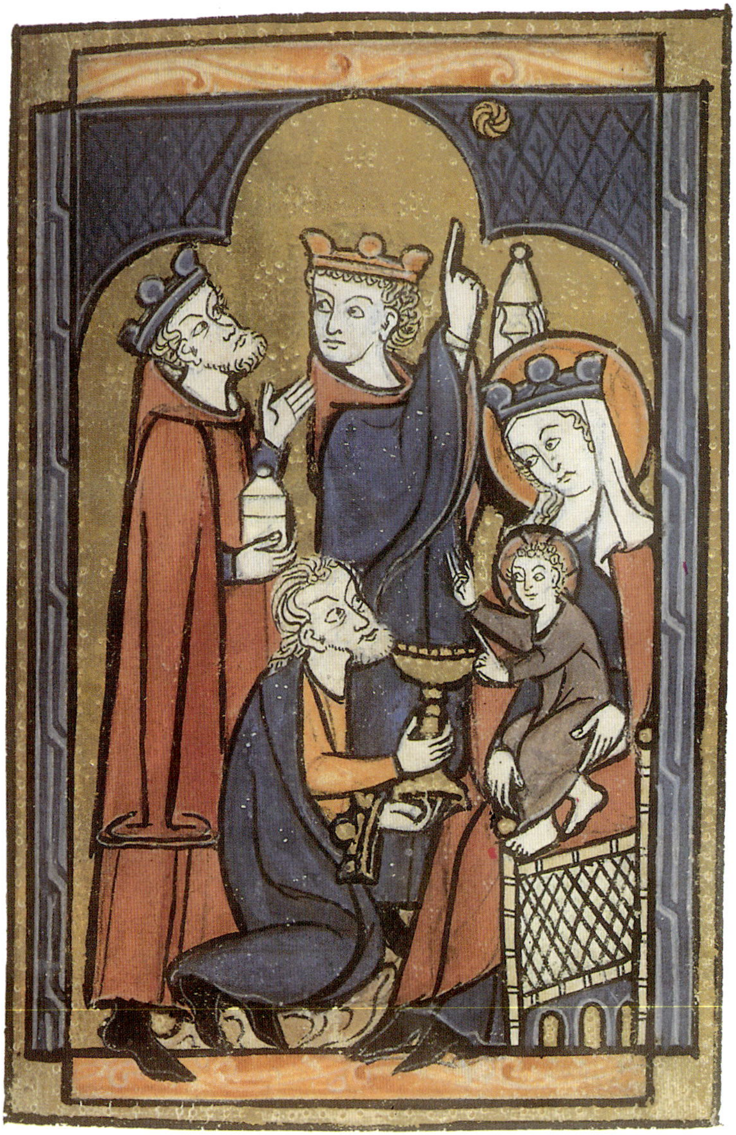

# December

23

24

25

26

27

28

29

*Above.* King David and his musicians praising God, from a late 14th-century psalter.

*Opposite.* The Adoration of the Magi from an English prayerbook, late 13th century.

## December

### 30

### 31

The familiar story of 'Puss in Boots' in a French edition of 1844.

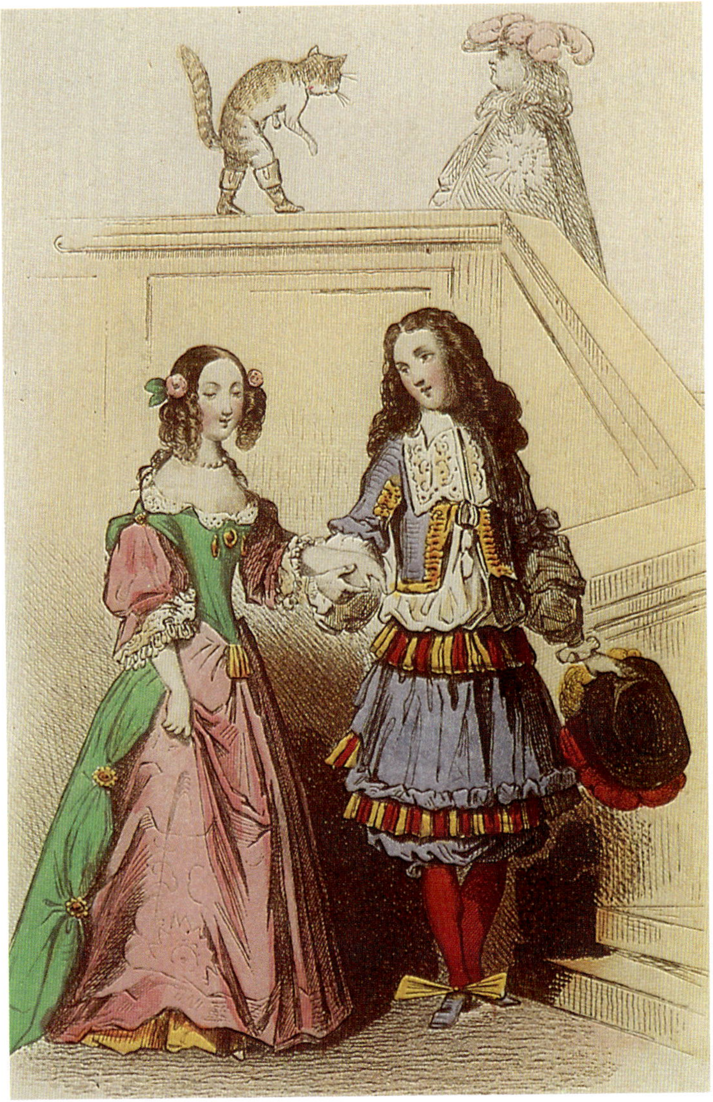

# Sources

### Cover illustration
Robert J. Thornton, *New Illustration of the sexual System of Carolus von Linnaeus*. London, 1807. FB.el. 47

### Frontispiece
The Lindsay Armorial, 1542. Adv. MS. 31.4.3

### Introduction
Sir Walter Scott's Magnum Opus, 1829–32. MSS. 23003, 23006–8.

The Chepman and Myllar Prints. Edinburgh, 1508. Sa. 6

### January
Georgio Calapoda, Portolan of the Mediterranean and Atlantic sea coasts, 1560. MS. 20995

Victorian scrap album, c. 1870. Mas. 1080

R. L. Stevenson, *A Child's Garden of Verses*. London, 1896. NG. 1168. b.1

*The High History of the Holy Graal*, translated by S. Evans. London, 1903. Bdg. m.122

Letter of Burns to Agnes McLehose, 1791. MS. 586, f.32

*Poems, chiefly in the Scottish Dialect*. Kilmarnock, 1786. RB. s.65

### February
*Serie delle Diverse Specie di Bastimenti da Guerra e Mercantili che navigano nel Mediterraneo*. [Engravings. By G. Tagliagambe. Italy, early 19th cent.] X. 21.a

Charles Rennie Mackintosh, *Haus eines Kunstfreundes*. (Meister der Innen Kunst, 2.) Darmstadt, [1902]. FB.el. 104

Annie B. Hore, *To Lake Tanganyika in a Bath Chair*. London, 1886. K. 128.e

James Hannington, *Peril and Adventure in Central Africa*. London, [1886]. K. 128.g

Michel Bouquet, *Scotland. The Tourist's Rambles in the Highlands*. Paris, [c. 1850]. L. 232.a

### March
Antiphoner. Italy, c. 1460. MS. 25241

Victorian scrap album. 19th cent. Mas. 1073

Agnes Miller Parker, *Fox: a wood-engraving*. Kansas City, 1941. FB. 1. 225

Illustration by A. M. Parker from *The Saturday Book, 1941–42*. London, 1941. T. 161.a

*Vues remarquables des Montagnes de la Suisse*. Amsterdam, 1785. GB/C.23

Book of Hours. Padua, 15th century. MS. 9742.

Watercolour by John Francis Campbell of Islay, 1850. Adv.MS. 50.3.17, f.74

*The Florist's Journal*, vol. 3. August 1842. M.101

### April
*New Dissected Maps: Europe*. [N.p., 1908]. Map Cur. 3

The Murthly Hours. England, late 13th and 14th cent. MS. 21000

"Kargo" (or "Card Golf"). London, [?1930]. Mas. 1163

*The Battle of Culloden*. [Engraving.] London, 1746. L. 197.c

### May
Dante Gabriel Rossetti, *The Blessed Damozel*. London and Edinburgh, [1913]. RB. s.1295

*Breviarium Romanum*. Venice, 1478. Inc. 118

The Hours of Marie de Rieux. France, 15th cent. Dep. 221/2

Jean de la Fontaine, *Fables*, vol. 1. Paris, 1838. JB. 510

Album of Walter Reid, c. 1860–70. Acc. 8621

Joan Blaeu, *Novum ac magnum theatrum urbium Belgicae foederatae*. Amsterdam, [1649]. Bart. Dep

*Quadrilles parées costumées éxécutées à la Cour de Sa Majesté le Roi de Bavière*. Munich, [1835]. FB. 1. 239

James Freebairn, *L'Eloge d'Ecosse*. Edinburgh, 1727. Ry. II. c. 37

The Album Amicorum of Sir Michael Balfour. Italy, 1596–9. MS. 16000

### June
Manoel de Andrade de Figueyredo, *Nova Escola para aprender a ler, escrever, & contar*. Lisbon, [1722]. ICAS. F4

Sir Walter Scott's Magnum Opus, 1829–32. MSS. 23003, 23006–8

M. E[gerton], *Airy Nothings... by Olio Rigmaroll*. London, 1825. FB.m. 150

The Album Amicorum of Sir Michael Balfour. Italy, 1596–9. MS. 16000

### July
Ordnance Survey tourist maps. Deeside, Thames, Chichester, Oban, Snowdon and the Peak District. [1920s]. Map Library

*The Calligraphic Models of Ludovico degli Arrighi surnamed Vicentino: a complete Facsimile*. Paris, 1926. X. 183.g

Miniature from a Book of Hours. France, c. 1500. MS. 8999

J. G. Hamilton, *Picturesque Delineations of the Highlands of Scotland*. London, 1825. RB. 1. 73

Frank Oates, *Matabele Land and the Victoria Falls*. Second edition. London, 1889. K.128. c

James Malton, *A Picturesque and Descriptive View of the City of Dublin*. London, [after 1802]. FB.el. 102

Album of Walter Reid, c. 1860–70. Acc. 9032

### August
*The Royal Primer: an Leabhar-chloinne rioghail*. Edinburgh, [187-]. H.M. 221

Abraham Ortelius, *Theatrum orbis terrarum*. Antwerp, 1592. WD. 2.0

Willem Blaeu, *Atlas maior*, vol. 1. Amsterdam, 1665. WD. 3.B

*The Cats' "At Home"*. Music by H. P. Danks. London, [1879]. Mus. Vol. 594(2)

Sir William Hamilton, *Campi Phlegraei: Observations on the Volcanos of the two Sicilies*. Naples, 1776. FB. 1. 78

Painting by a Jaipur artist, c. 1820. MS. 16487

SEPTEMBER
Thomas Brown, *Illustrations of the American Ornithology of Alexander Wilson and Charles Lucian Bonaparte*. Edinburgh, 1835. FB.el. 21

Drawing by John Harden, 1809. MS. 8866, I.16

Thomas Brown, *Illustrations of the American Ornithology of Alexander Wilson and Charles Lucian Bonaparte*. Edinburgh, 1835. FB.el. 21

OCTOBER
*The International Struggle between England, Scotland, Ireland, France & America*. [Poster.] Edinburgh, 1887. Weir 7(27)

The Forman Armorial, c. 1562. Adv. MS. 31.4.2

Notebook of James Ferguson, 1742. Acc. 10254/1. Also James Ferguson, *A new Globe of the Earth*. [London, c. 1750]. Map Cur. 6

Alexander Lockhart, *Disputatio juridica*. Edinburgh, 1774. Bdg. s.24

Aleph, *Geographical Fun*. London, [1869]. E.125.a

NOVEMBER
*Le Cabinet des Modes*, vol. 3. [Paris], 1787–8. FB. s.182

Petrus Kaerius, *Leo Belgicus*. From Petrus Montanus, *La Germanie inférieure*. Amsterdam, 1622. Newb. 4412

Detail from *T'Klooster St Aechten* in Joan Blaeu, *Novum ac magnum theatrum urbium Belgicae foederatae*. Amsterdam, [1649]. Bart. Dep.

James Hannington, *Peril and Adventure in Central Africa*. London, [1886]. K. 128.g

DECEMBER
E. A. de Cosson, *The Cradle of the Blue Nile*, vol. 1. London, 1877. K. 128.e

Letter of Mary, Queen of Scots, to Henri III of France, 1587. Adv. MS. 54.1.1

John Leslie, *Du Droict et Tiltre de... Marie Royne d'Ecosse*. Rouen, [1587]. Ry. III. d.33

Album of prints and drawings collected in Italy, c. 1827. MS. 5791

The Murthly Hours. England, late 13th and 14th cent. MS. 21000

The Bohun Psalter. England, late 14th cent. Adv. MS. 18.6.5

Charles Perrault, *Les Contes de Fées*. Paris, [1844]. Campbell 2.a